Maggie Rowe has written a masterpiece—her magnum opus—and will guide you through evaluating your inner journey with all its anxiety, insecurity, and pain. She'll teach you how to live an intentional, purposeful life that's filled with relationships that matter. The focus of this book isn't becoming perfect—it's being God-focused and infusing your life with transformational truth. The writing is exquisite, and each reflection will challenge you to live a life that matters. You can read this book on your own, but if you want to grow a deeper spiritual relationship with a friend, ask her to join you on this journey.

CAROL KENT, speaker; author of *He Holds My Hand*

This Life We Share is a wonderfully comprehensive guide for those who want to live and love well with God, people, and the world. With wisdom born from a deep faith, a broad knowledge of Scripture, and a life well lived, Maggie serves the reader as a trusted life coach in these pages. Grab a few friends and journey together as you engage her words. You'll be glad that you did.

SCOTT SAULS, senior pastor of Christ Presbyterian Church; author of several books, including *Jesus Outside the Lines* and *Irresistible Faith*

The beauty of a book written by a wise older woman is that there is something for everyone—a lifetime of varied adventures and challenges which affirm the goodness of God. Every page of *This Life We Share* reminds me that life with God and others is indeed a treasure. Please savor Maggie Rowe's words slowly, that the rich truth might sink deeply into your soul, offering strength for your own journey.

LUCINDA SECREST McDOWELL, speaker; author of *Soul Strong* and *Life-Giving Choices*

Maggie Rowe has never steered me wrong, and her insights and great humor as well as spiritual compass on true north have always informed all her advice. As they do this book. Take it from me—follow Maggie's direction, as it is based on Christ's. Read this book.

HUGH HEWITT, author, journalist, syndicated Salem Radio Network host

The first time I met Maggie Rowe, I knew she was special. A woman of deep wisdom, unending kindness, seemingly effortless generosity, and a ten-mile-deep love for God and others. In this memoir of her spiritual journey, Maggie transforms her own life-lived-well into a map for the rest of us. Here are fifty-two devotional reflections filled with kindness, generosity, and the sort of wisdom that can transform you from your "everyday" self into the person you actually want to be. Buy this book, read it, and find in it some quiet space for your heart to soar.

SANDRA RICHTER, Robert H. Gundry Chair of Biblical Studies at Westmont College; author of *The Epic of Eden*

Bravo to Maggie Wallem Rowe! Maggie is honest, vulnerable, and exhibiting of grace. She provides fifty-two reflections through which all the biggies shine—womanhood, motherhood, pastor's-wife-hood, Scripture studenthood, and writer/actress-hood. You will know Maggie. And that is a blessing because you may know yourself better.

DIKKON EBERHART, PhD, author of *The Time Mom Met Hitler, Frost Came to Dinner, and I Heard the Greatest Story Ever Told*

As I traveled through the pages of this book, I was enchanted by Maggie's vivid descriptions, her honest longings to do life better, and her genuine love for all who read her words. I soon realized that Maggie's story is my story, and most likely your story. *This Life We Share* is filled with time-honored truths for all generations. We, the readers, are the beneficiaries as Maggie shares her life, connects us with biblical stories, and points us to the one who guides our every step. This is a book to read and reread, and most definitely to share with others.

CYNTHIA FANTASIA, DMin, speaker; author of *In the Lingering Light*

Maggie has spent decades following Jesus—as a pastor's wife, coworker, mother, daughter, and friend. Now she puts pen to page to share the wisdom she's learned along the way. Maggie has a gift for seeing the world and finding meaning in ordinary days, capturing it in delightful prose. She also has the gift of insight, the ability to harness her own self-awareness for the good of others. In this book, you'll find more than good advice; I expect you'll find a new friend.

CARMEN JOY IMES, associate professor of Old Testament at Prairie College; author of *Bearing God's Name*

In *This Life We Share*, Maggie Rowe has provided weary Christian women with rich, soul-nourishing words that sink down deep. Engaging with these brief but substantive reflections feels like going on a road trip with a best friend.

STEVE WIENS, author of *Shining like the Sun*, *Beginnings*, and *Whole*

This Life We Share is an encouraging read about navigating life events in light of scriptural insight. As a cherished sister in Christ, Maggie takes the reader through her own circumstances, fusing her knowledge of God's Word alongside essential wisdom, humor, and truth. Here, Maggie has created a work that is both challenging to the reader and reassuring—ever pointing toward Christ, who has gone before us.

REBECCA VAN DEN BRINK, pastor of ministries at North Sea Baptist Church, Stavanger, Norway

Only a sensitive observer could have written this book. I have enjoyed Maggie's deep insights and ability to synthesize life's challenges and joys for over thirty years. She is a student of people, Scripture, biography, herself, and those she loves, and an eager friend. In short, wherever she is, Maggie is all there. It would be difficult to name a subject women might face that this book doesn't describe and handle with vulnerability, honesty, humor, and understanding. I can imagine a small group of women bonding very easily as they glean more about life from Maggie's wisdom and decades of experience. Hard questions? Bring them on!

GAIL MacDONALD, wife, mom, grandmother, friend; author of *High Call, High Privilege*

What if you had a mentor, a sister willing to share the wisdom she's learned along life's way? With her book *This Life We Share*, author Maggie Rowe is exactly that. From impostor syndrome to immigration to infertility, Maggie offers bite-size nuggets of wisdom to encourage you to keep walking forward on this shared journey of life.

CATHERINE McNIEL, author of *Long Days of Small Things* and *All Shall Be Well*

MAGGIE WALLEM ROWE

This Life We Share

52 reflections on journeying well with God and others

NavPress

A NavPress resource published in alliance
with Tyndale House Publishers

NavPress is the publishing ministry of The Navigators, an international Christian organization and leader in personal spiritual development. NavPress is committed to helping people grow spiritually and enjoy lives of meaning and hope through personal and group resources that are biblically rooted, culturally relevant, and highly practical.

For more information, visit NavPress.com.

This Life We Share: 52 Reflections on Journeying Well with God and Others

Copyright © 2020 by Marjorie W. Rowe. All rights reserved.

A NavPress resource published in alliance with Tyndale House Publishers

NAVPRESS and the NavPress logo are registered trademarks of NavPress, The Navigators, Colorado Springs, CO. *TYNDALE* is a registered trademark of Tyndale House Publishers. Absence of ® in connection with marks of NavPress or other parties does not indicate an absence of registration of those marks.

The Team:
Don Pape, Publisher
Caitlyn Carlson, Acquisitions Editor
Elizabeth Schroll, Copy Editor
Jacqueline L. Nuñez, Designer

Cover illustration of watercolor sunrise and leaves copyright © Liia Chevnenko/Shutterstock. All rights reserved.

Author photo by Mary Denman Photography © 2019. All rights reserved.

All Scripture quotations, unless otherwise indicated, are taken from the Holy Bible, *New International Version,*® *NIV.*® Copyright © 1973, 1978, 1984, 2011 by Biblica, Inc.® Used by permission. All rights reserved worldwide. Scripture quotations marked CEV are taken from the Contemporary English Version, copyright © 1991, 1992, 1995 by American Bible Society. Used by permission. Scripture quotations marked KJV are taken from the *Holy Bible*, King James Version. Scripture quotations marked MSG are taken from *THE MESSAGE*, copyright © 1993, 2002, 2018 by Eugene H. Peterson. Used by permission of NavPress. All rights reserved. Represented by Tyndale House Publishers. Scripture quotations marked NASB are taken from the New American Standard Bible,® copyright © 1960, 1962, 1963, 1968, 1971, 1972, 1973, 1975, 1977, 1995 by The Lockman Foundation. Used by permission. Scripture quotations marked NCV are taken from the New Century Version.® Copyright © 2005 by Thomas Nelson, Inc. Used by permission. All rights reserved. Scripture quotations marked NKJV are taken from the New King James Version,® copyright © 1982 by Thomas Nelson, Inc. Used by permission. All rights reserved. Scripture quotations marked NLT are taken from the *Holy Bible*, New Living Translation, copyright © 1996, 2004, 2015 by Tyndale House Foundation. Used by permission of Tyndale House Publishers, Carol Stream, Illinois 60188. All rights reserved.

Some of the anecdotal illustrations in this book are true to life and are included with the permission of the persons involved. Some names have been changed to protect privacy. All other illustrations are composites of real situations, and any resemblance to people living or dead is purely coincidental.

For information about special discounts for bulk purchases, please contact Tyndale House Publishers at csresponse@tyndale.com, or call 1-800-323-9400.

ISBN 978-1-64158-007-6

Printed in the United States of America

26	25	24	23	22	21	20
7	6	5	4	3	2	1

To Michael

First reader, first everything.

You believed in me when I never believed in myself.

I am grateful beyond words for the life we share.

Contents

Foreword

A couple of summers ago, I stood on a bridge over a rushing section of the river on one of the branches of the Connecticut River in rural Vermont. There were rocks below, and the water was cascading toward me in wild motion below my feet. Had I been in the river, I would have been swept downstream in a moment. But I stood safely above, leaning over the railing that faced upstream. The water rushed beneath me and on past me with a steady chorus of white noise, and I thought of how fast life comes toward us like the river: circumstances, emotion, and decisions that need to be made in a hurry.

The bridge was about twenty-five feet wide from rail to rail. I strolled across to the other side and noticed a change. It was quiet on the south side of the bridge. I could hear over the ripples, and I felt stilled, reflecting and pondering.

Moments of pause are so important to help us see the big picture clearly. When life tumbles over us like rushing water, our substantive life, the good stuff of who we really are, rests beneath the changing currents. We are sturdy, like the rocks of the riverbed, weathering the elements in flood and drought.

Maggie Wallem Rowe leads us into those quiet places in deeper waters. She takes us back to what matters, like a trusted friend. Her words read like a deep breath. Turning over the subjects of shame, calling, truth telling, fear, and friendship, she offers each reflection graciously, not as heavy-handed devotionals but thoughtful considerations. Though the passages may be brief, they stay with you, these moments of pause in a rushing-water life.

My songwriter friend says that every good song follows an invisible map of what it means to go out on a journey and to return home. As I write this, I have four more days of travel before I can rest at my home in Tennessee, but while I am away, I find that I am tethered by small, liturgical gestures of morning coffee, evening prayers from the prayer book, and a call to check in with my husband in the afternoon.

At the pace of our world, in the midst of the clamor of technology, there is a great need to cultivate reflection. Racing from one thing to another, we are hounded by advertisements and appointments. It's hard to tell what is most important in light of what is urgent.

Daily rhythms and slowness like the kind that Maggie Rowe offers here have been a saving grace for me when life is full to the brim. In the deep breaths overlooking the river, she gives us the space to recast a fresh vision for this shared life.

Sandra McCracken
singer-songwriter

Introduction

"Let's take a road trip!"

These five words were the catalyst for some of the best experiences of my childhood. I grew up on a farm in north-central Illinois, and while I have sunny memories of rural life, the work never stopped for my hardworking parents. There were cows that needed milking twice daily; sheep, chickens, and pigs to tend; and hundreds of acres of soybeans and seed corn to be cultivated, planted, and harvested.

On the rare occasions when my father felt we could get away, the five of us piled in our red four-door sedan with the 1960s fins, humming the jingle "See the USA in your Chevrolet!" My siblings and I were part of the postwar baby boom, but minivans hadn't been invented yet. Or seat belts.

The three of us jostled for space in the back seat, my long-legged older sister next to one window and my easygoing little brother perched on a cushion by the other so he could see out. As the skinny middle child, I was wedged in between, straddling the hump on the floor while poking and provoking them with my sharp-elbowed peevishness. Maggie-in-the-middle was not anyone's idea of a preferred travel companion. We always got to our destination, but I'm sure I didn't make it fun.

Unless you're prone to motion sickness, restless legs, or cranky companions, most of us enjoy road trips. We don't always get to choose our travel mates, but we do get to decide how to behave ourselves. Sometimes we're still like kids on the journey, focusing more on our present discomfort ("Are we there yet?") than on our final destination.

Life has its epic adventures, but the dailiness of it doesn't consist of grand moments. Rather, we live in the everyday rhythms of the intentional choices we make. Paying attention to our mental, emotional, and spiritual health. Caring for others and being cared for in return. Loving God and receiving his unconditional love and fathomless grace.

I still love to travel, and I always will. But if there's one person I've occasionally wished I could leave behind at a rest stop, it hasn't been a sibling or my spouse, coworkers, or friends. It's myself. Dang, the times I would have liked to jettison the old, scrappy Maggie for a new, vastly improved edition! A girl who could be consistently kind and thoughtful. A teen confident enough in her own skin to reach out to others. A woman not beset by anxiety and insecurity about what others thought of her and whether she would ever measure up.

The words ahead of you have been birthed out of many soul struggles in my life—moments when I thought I had to be the only person still wrestling with fear and self-doubt, a propensity to worry rather than trust, or the temptation to measure my weaknesses against others' strengths. But God and his children met me in the midst of my questions. The chapters in my story have been punctuated with disjointed grammatical constructions: the comma experiences that forced me to wait; the period places that came to a full stop; and the exclamation points of pure, unexpected joy.

In the decades following those fractious childhood trips, I've written thousands of words in journals, diaries, and blog posts describing what I've been learning about myself, God, and traveling well with others on this shared journey called life. I've collected a lifetime of notes strewn like white pebbles on the paths I've taken. The book you hold is the result.

I'm now a seasoned life traveler in my third trimester of living on this side of eternity. Birth into new life might be a few decades or only years away. I feel the weight of it, the aching and longing for a future I can only imagine. But like any woman carrying something infinitely precious to her, I am fiercely passionate about birthing what God has given me over my life's gestation on this planet. The readings, questions, and LifeLines you'll find in these pages contain transformational stories and principles I've experienced in over a half century of knowing and loving God.

There are fifty-two reflections you can read in whatever order you choose. Just as a new element sometimes needs to be introduced into a situation to produce change, perhaps these readings can serve as a catalyst for your own growth, to forge fresh soul connections with your traveling companions and the God whose presence is infused in every moment of your journey.

If you are wondering what a mentor might say about growing spiritually when you have neither quiet nor time, sink into reflection 34. Or maybe you are wrestling with emotions that need validation or a loving confrontation; join me in reflection 28. If a day comes when you have questions about marriage, turn to reflections 31 or 32 for coaching. And in a season of sorrow, when you need to know that God is not unaware of your pain and your feelings of sadness, find encouragement in reflection 6. You don't need to resign yourself to going it alone. This life is meant to be lived in community.

Because *This Life We Share* is designed to help you make new soul connections, consider finding someone to journey through these reflections with you. You might already be part of a small group or a book club, but if not, consider inviting a coworker or the neighbor down the hall or across the street to join you. Human relationships are richest and sweetest when grounded in spiritual realities: As each person's vertical dimension points toward God, robust horizontal connections form.

"Two people are better off than one," a well-known passage from Ecclesiastes reminds us, "for they can help each other succeed."[1] Whether we call it discipleship, mentoring, or simply friendship forged in faith, making soul connections with others who are journeying toward God will inevitably strengthen our own walk—and make the friendship stronger.

But perhaps you've just relocated or are entering a new season of life where you don't know a soul to confide in. I've been there, too, many times. Whether you're feeling alone or surrounded by traveling companions, I'd love to come alongside you in this life we share.

You are dearly loved, and *you are not alone.*

Maggie Wallem Rowe
PEACE RIDGE
WWW.MAGGIEROWE.COM

PART I

The Inner Journey

A great traveler . . . is a kind of introspective;
as he covers the ground outwardly,
so he advances fresh interpretations of himself inwardly.

LAWRENCE DURRELL, QUOTED IN DAVID YEADON,
The Way of the Wanderer

DURING THE YEARS MY HUSBAND, Mike, served as a youth pastor, he often asked the students he worked with to memorize the second chapter of Philippians. When the teens were preparing for short-term mission trips or service projects, committing Philippians 2 to heart was a requirement.

Mike's reasoning was simple. In this particular passage of Scripture, the apostle Paul is exhorting the people of Philippi to agree wholeheartedly with each other, love one another, and work together with one mind and purpose. In our teenage years, many of us are not yet mature enough to consistently do these things. Learning Paul's instructions before departing on a mission trip was a key step in these teens' spiritual and emotional development.

There's a fundamental phrase, though, embedded within Paul's instruction: "Don't look out *only* for your own interests."[1] While reminding his readers to take a genuine interest in others, the apostle naturally assumes we'll tend to our own needs too.

In order to live well with others, we need to pay close attention to our own mental and emotional health first. Our feelings do matter, deeply. They are us: "Emotion is not the Cinderella of our inner life, to be kept in her place among the cinders in the kitchen. Our emotional life is *us* in a way our intellectual life cannot be."[2] A woman or man who deeply desires to be useful to others must build from the inside out. The life hidden within each of us determines our responses to the daily complexities of life.

Some may disagree, but I don't believe that happiness—or any other emotional state, for that matter—is a choice. We can no more legislate how we feel at any given moment than we can control the waves of the ocean. But while we can't choose our feelings, we *can* choose what to do with those feelings. The unseen weather of the heart makes a dramatic impact when it comes ashore in other people's lives. Social commentator Andy Rooney once observed, "When you harbor bitterness, happiness will dock elsewhere."[3] The same can be said of most negativity. God has given us the agency to respond to what is in our hearts, and he's not left us to manage either the marvels or the messes of our lives alone.

In the pages ahead, we'll look at some of the twists and turns of our inner journey. The Word of God will serve as our map as we navigate the uncertain terrain of seeking peace amid suffering, dealing with fears about the future, and managing anxiety and worry. We'll identify ways we can elect to respond with hope even when joy seems elusive or when we despair of God ever using our broken stories.

You are the only one who can traverse all the hidden pathways of your inner journey. But in this beautiful life we share, I'm here to offer you a walking stick, a water bottle, and warm companionship along the way. Your heart, like a compass, is already pointed toward Home.

TOO MUCH TO DO

The apostles then rendezvoused with Jesus and reported on all that they had done and taught. Jesus said, "Come off by yourselves; let's take a break and get a little rest." For there was constant coming and going. They didn't even have time to eat.

MARK 6:30-31, MSG

DO YOU EVER FEEL LIKE YOU'RE LIVING your life inside a blender with the button stuck on Pulse?

When my husband, Mike, and I started out in ministry over forty years ago, advice for clergy families focused on surviving life in the fishbowl. Those were the days when pastors' families usually lived in a parsonage or manse that was either attached to the church or located nearby.

Mike's aunt Alice recalls the time she and her pastor-husband, Russ, lived in an apartment in the back of a Methodist church in rural Pennsylvania. A door behind the organ in the back of the sanctuary led directly into their quarters. Early one Sunday morning, Russ forgot to relock it after he left early to prepare for the service. Alice was ironing in their kitchen, wearing nothing but her slip, when a parishioner walked in, looking to borrow utensils.

"I didn't mind living in a fishbowl," Alice says, laughing, "but I preferred to do it with my clothes on!"

Family life today resembles more a blender than a fishbowl. The problem is not so much that others are watching us but that we're barely keeping up with ourselves. We are exhausted from the continual whirl of family, volunteer, and work responsibilities. Our lives are running on high speed, and we have little hope of either slowing down or catching up.

Do you have more than one email account to monitor? How about a status to update, networking requests to approve, and social-media posts to keep current? Even email doesn't move fast enough for some. Want to stay in touch with your kids? Better text or use their favorite app.

Technology has blurred the boundaries between night and day, work and home. Think you're caught up when you leave the office at 5 or 6 p.m.? Not when colleagues desperate to empty their own inboxes dump documents and dilemmas on your virtual desk all night long.

When we live life at blender speed, is there any Off button? With so many needs to care for, how do we connect with the needs of our own souls? I use a "3-D" concept that works well much of the time: decide, delegate, and delete.

Decide what's really important. Sounds obvious, doesn't it?

Greek, the language of the New Testament, uses two distinct words for our English concept of time. *Chronos*, from which we derive the word *chronology*, is clock time. Each of us has the same amount: twenty-four hours in a day. *Kairos* is human time, the time we make and take for our purposes. *Chronos* is a given determined by God, but *kairos* is a moral choice we make every hour of the day.

When our kids were young and I worked out of our home on

Cape Cod, I gladly relinquished their care to their dad as soon as he arrived home each evening. While Mike and the kids read or played, I hopped on the computer to prepare talks or plan conferences for the regional ministry I directed. Nothing guilt-inducing there. Our family functioned as a team, and teams make trade-offs.

One evening, I was about to return a long list of calls when I glanced out the kitchen window, arrested by the sight of snow drifting down as the kids lobbed snowballs at their dad. They were shrieking with joy, but I was missing out. Dropping the phone, I pulled on boots and a jacket and hurried outside. Later that night, as Mike tucked our eight-year-old into bed, Adam looked up with shining eyes and said, "Dad, we had the *bestest* time when Mom came out!"

How easily I could have missed that moment. How often have I missed others?

Delegate. I know—easy to say and hard to do. We feel like we're imposing when we ask others to handle responsibilities, or we fear the task won't be done right—if it's done at all. When we're living life at blender speed, it seems easier to just do things ourselves.

But we trust toddlers with certain tasks—picking up their toys, putting on their shoes. We should be able to trust big people too. Delegation is key to mentoring and mothering, both. How do we do it? By providing others the opportunity to do a task, the authority to carry it out, the skills or training necessary, and the accountability that comes with faithful follow-up.

Delete. Remember the old clunker about home organization: "If in doubt, throw it out"? Those words apply to more than possessions. A schedule crowded with morning-to-midnight commitments leaves no room for the spiritual formation that needs to take place in our inner being. In her description of living for a time among the Amish, writer Sue Bender commented, "The Amish often leave a space, a seeming mistake in the midst of their well-thought-out plans, to serve as an opening to let the spirit come in."[1]

Is living life at blender speed making you nauseated? Even blenders have different settings and slower speeds. Decide what God would have you and *only* you do in this season of your life. Delete other activities; delegate the rest. In *Lean In*, Facebook COO Sheryl Sandberg's bestselling book on women in leadership, Sandberg writes that the coining of the phrase "having it all" is perhaps "the greatest trap ever set for women. . . . These three little words are intended to be aspirational but instead make all of us feel like we have fallen short."[2]

Life pulses with opportunities, but we don't have to embrace them all at one time. There's more to life than increasing its speed.

Points of Connection

1. Can you identify with the Mark 6:30-31 account of the apostles, who were dealing with so much coming and going that they didn't even have time to eat? How can Jesus' advice to his followers apply to the pace of your life today? Consider some practical ways you can carve out five minutes of quiet a day, an hour each week, or a day each month.

2. When she's out of the office, my friend Robin sometimes leaves an out-of-office message indicating she won't be answering calls or emails while on vacation: "Know phone, no peace. No phone, know peace." If you're not in a position to totally unplug, what measures can you take to guard the margins in your life?

3. A simple prayer based on Ephesians 5:15 that has helped me might become yours, as well: "Lord, show me how to use my time wisely and well."

Life pulses with opportunities,
but we don't have to embrace them all at the same time.

KICK ANXIETY TO THE CURB

Don't fret or worry. Instead of worrying, pray. Let petitions and praises
shape your worries into prayers, letting God know your concerns.
Before you know it, a sense of God's wholeness, everything coming
together for good, will come and settle you down. It's wonderful what
happens when Christ displaces worry at the center of your life.

PHILIPPIANS 4:6-7, MSG

BENT OVER MY WORK COMPUTER, I glanced up occasionally through
the eight-foot plate-glass window in my office to study the enormous black storm clouds boiling up from the southwest. *I'd like to*
get home before that hits, I thought.

Only it didn't.

Umbrella in hand at 5:00 p.m., I gathered my things, only to
note with astonishment the brilliant light now pouring through my
office window. That storm I wanted to beat home? Never arrived.

Sometimes the things we fear never do.

A handwringer by nature, I've spent a lifetime trying to distin-
guish worry from its sibling, concern. They share a family resemblance, after all. Both are kin to care. Each has its ancestry in the
state of apprehension.

How do you separate these conjoined twins?

When I reentered the corporate workforce in a new profession at age fifty-three, I sat at my desk the first morning, staring at my computer, wondering whether I'd ever learn enough to truly be useful. Caring enough to work hard, to strive to reward the confidence of those who hired me? That was totally legit. But worrying about failure? Futile. I printed out a simple sign in big block letters to remind myself that every day I learned something new would be a good day at work.

Every corner of life provides something to worry about—family medical crises, financial pressures, once-valued relationships that have slipped out of sight. These are all things I care deeply about—situations where I have to choose, over and over, between worry and concern.

Worry has likely waggled his fingers in your face more than once. He's the playground bully who pokes and prods and steals peace of mind as if he could spend it for lunch. So how do we kick worry to the curb? How do we choose the responsibility of concern without the anxiety of worry?

- **Talk it out.** Verbally process your concerns. Seek information and talk it through with trusted advisors. Talk to medical personnel, your pastor, or a counselor. Take notes; seek second opinions. Take your dark thoughts on long walks to expose them to the light. Pour out your pain to God.

- **Resist the rut.** Someone described persistent worry as carving a rut into which all other thoughts drain. Once you've processed your concerns and taken them to those who are in a position to help, *switch lanes.* What you fear most might well run off into the ditch before it ever reaches you.

- **Pay attention to the positive.** It's there, you know. That half-full glass. The loved one who is getting better. That friend with stage 4 cancer who has a 50 percent *survival* rate. The marriage that might improve or dissolve but in either case will not leave the suffering spouse in limbo forever.

I have an awful habit of inquiring anxiously, "Is everything all right?" when one of my kids calls unexpectedly. They know me well enough to laugh and say, "Yeah, Mom, everything's fine."

But you know what? The next time a call comes, I'm gonna choose to say, "Hey, what's new and good today?"

What you fear may never arrive. But even if it does, you can still kick worry to the curb. Let him go bully someone else. Or better yet, come alongside another worrier and put your arm through theirs. Then link both your arms through God's.

Worry loses its power when you face the bully together.

Points of Connection

1. "Don't fret or worry." Easier said than done, right? Read Philippians 4:6-7 through several times, pausing after each phrase. How can our petitions and praises shape our worries into prayers?

2. Picture the situation you're worried about as a huge beach ball. How much of it can you see at any time? If you walk around it in prayer, does your angle of vision change your perspective? Read what 2 Corinthians 4:16-18 has to say about a change in spiritual perspective.

3. Prayer is a powerful soul connection between friends. Ask someone to partner with you. If the first person you ask isn't available, keep looking! You could be the answer to someone else's desire for a prayer partner. When you find each other, agree together on your petitions and sign them with the name of Jesus as you offer them to God.

Life Line

Worry and concern can feel like conjoined twins, but prayer has the power to sever the connection.

WHEN YOU DON'T FEEL GOOD ENOUGH

In a well-furnished kitchen there are not only crystal goblets and silver platters, but waste cans and compost buckets—some containers used to serve fine meals, others to take out the garbage. Become the kind of container God can use to present any and every kind of gift to his guests for their blessing.

2 TIMOTHY 2:20-21, MSG

YOU WERE UP FOR A JOB PROMOTION, and it went to someone else. That audition for the role in the play or the seat in the orchestra? You gave it your best, but the director chose another. You knew you had the leadership position that fit your qualifications to a T, as in Too Perfect—until the next in line got the nod.

Why should she be chosen when you know you've got the talent, the experience, the credentials? Were you too young or too old? The wrong color or dress size? Maybe they thought you voted for the wrong party in the past election. Ageism, sexism, racism, partisan politics—all the reasons we get passed over. It's infuriating and unfair.

In an episode of the popular television drama *This Is Us*,[1] Pearson sister Kate screws up her courage and attends a vocal audition, only to panic when she compares herself unfavorably to the other contestants. She flees before her number is called.

In the restaurant where her brother Kevin and her boyfriend, Toby, are waiting, Kate admits she chickened out—only to have the guys argue about whose job it is to comfort or encourage her. Kate finally explodes: "I'm a thirty-seven-year-old woman! I shouldn't need to be pushed or coddled—not by a man, not by a husband, not by a brother, not by anyone." Returning to the audition, Kate insists they give her a chance, even if she is significantly larger than the other women competing for the lead. Surprised, the director listens as she sings beautifully—only to dismiss her after a few measures.

Furious and not about to accept discrimination, Kate launches into a tirade of protest. The director interrupts, asking the backup singer to step forward and cover the same song Kate began. She's fabulous.

"That's Amber," the director says in frustration. "She's our backup singer. She was our lead singer, but we demoted her because she wasn't good enough. . . . I don't care what dress size you wear. You're not good enough, honey."

It's tempting to assume someone else got the gig we wanted because the system is rigged, or she had connections, or he had an edge because of his race. But you know what? Sometimes we don't get picked simply because we're not good enough. Someone else's talents or skills exceed ours. Like Kate, we need to woman up and admit that in a competitive world, we can't all come in first. *And that's okay.*

Years ago, I worked in a department with few opportunities for advancement. No problem; it was a level playing field for all. Until the day a management position was created and a colleague with less seniority than I had got it.

Was I hurt? Sure was. I accepted the decision publicly, but privately I cried and—so mature of me—slammed a few drawers in my office while I was at it. Almost threw a vase at the window too.

But here's the thing. The coworker who was awarded that promotion? She had terrific management skills. Once I got over my internal hissy fit, I knew our entire team would benefit from her skills. It's not that I wasn't good at what I did. She was better, and I knew it. In the years to follow, I couldn't have been prouder of the stellar way she served our team.

The apostle Paul wrote that we're all vessels God can use, but our Creator did not make clones. Some of us shine in certain situations, while others fill less visible but equally important functions.

Maybe we're not all designed to be Waterford crystal, refracting the light and drawing the praise. Sometimes we're the compost bucket instead, the repository of what others have discarded.

But fancy crystal can be fragile, while that unremarkable compost bucket? Ah, the rich possibilities for fertilizing the lives of others!

Points of Connection

1. Is there a certain area of your life where you feel you don't measure up? Did someone else get the grades, the promotion, or the relationship you hoped for? Acknowledge the hurt. Talk to God about it. What could that experience make possible in your own life?

2. Jesus' disciples struggled with comparisons too. When Jesus reinstated Peter to service after the disciple's public denials, he also indicated the kind of death Peter could anticipate. Peter pointed to John and asked, "Lord, what about him?" only to

have Jesus reply, "If I want him to remain alive until I return, what is that to you? You must follow me" (John 21:21-22). The next time you're tempted to wonder why God might bless someone differently than he has blessed you, remember the WITTY principle: *What is that to you? Follow me.*

We all waste energy coveting the experiences and privileges others have. God has designed a unique path just for you. No one can walk it as well as you can.

SHEDDING THE SHAME

So now there is no condemnation for those who belong to Christ Jesus.

ROMANS 8:1, NLT

IT HAPPENED DECADES AGO, but the incident still causes bile to rise in my throat.

An individual convinced that my husband and I were on the wrong side of a church situation decided to harass us in any way possible, including stalking, sending hate mail, and worse. One winter night, I hurried home through our village, knowing the man was only a few steps behind me in the darkness. My heart was hammering, but I could still hear his low hissing: "Shame. Shame on you, Maggie!"

Past trauma takes powerful strokes when it breaks the surface of the unconscious mind.

I usually can't recall what I ate for dinner yesterday, but frightening experiences imprint on my memory like footprints on wet cement, quickly hardening to preserve what I'd rather forget.

Perhaps you've been there too. Whether you carry the shame of poor past choices or what others have inflicted on you, you know how it feels to have your face burn with unwanted and unbidden memories. Shame always emerges out of the dark.

Merriam-Webster Dictionary defines *shame* as "a painful emotion caused by consciousness of guilt, shortcoming, or impropriety."[1] When we are guilty of wrongdoing, shame is a legitimate response. Maybe years ago, when you tried to fit in at school, you joined in the mocking of another student. Or perhaps as a young adult, you took that which did not belong to you—someone else's possessions or significant other.

If we could exorcise the past by righting those wrongs, we would, but the memory of our actions remains. Shame.

And what of those who are made to feel ashamed when they themselves are the victims? People who have survived abuse were often threatened or intimidated into silence. The man who stalked us seemed to be projecting his shame over issues in his own life onto us. Even when there is no blame to take, shame holds on tightly. How can we ever force shame to release its grip?

Several years ago, I discovered a remarkable painting created by a Cistercian nun, Sister Grace Remington, simply titled *Virgin Mary Consoles Eve*.[2] This visual tale of two women depicts Eve, mother of mankind, covered by her hair, head bowed, bare legs bound in the coils of a snake. To her right stands Mary, womb great with child, her right arm reaching out to gently lift Eve's face while her bare foot crushes the head of the serpent.

Eve's story is told in the Book of Beginnings, where humankind's willful disobedience leads to eternal consequence: the serpent accursed and progeny forever at war. And then the powerful prophecy: "He will crush your head, and you will strike his heel."[3]

Mary's story is told in the Gospels, where we learn that a poor Jewish teenager has been chosen by God to bear a child who will bring salvation to the world.[4] Redemption would not be accomplished through Mary herself but rather through the one being woven together in her womb. Her son would become her Savior as well. One day, the mother would behold her Messiah.

Yet Sister Remington's painting reveals a powerful truth. The first woman, head bowed, faces the invisible Shame Lifter, the one who while riding in his mother's womb is already Redeemer of the world. The one who would proclaim during his earthly ministry that authority had been given to him over everything and everyone.[5] The one who would crush the head of the serpent sent to deceive, mislead, and shame God's people.

Did you wake up today feeling the serpent's fangs embedded in your hands, his coils wrapped around your heart? Is the enemy of your soul using every vulnerability from your past to pull you down in the present?

The lies of our accuser can be strident and powerful. More powerful still is the grace of the one who took the blame and bore the cost for our shame, whether or not we've had any part in its origin. Christ came as the fulfillment of the *protoevangelium*, "the first glimmer of the gospel,"[6] and he will not rest on our behalf until he has "put all his enemies under his feet."[7]

The wonderful truth is this: You and I no longer need to live under the crushing weight of shame. In Christ, we have been given the authority to shake off all that seeks to ensnare us.[8]

What a remarkable privilege we have! Immanuel, *God with us*,[9] has given us the power to lift our heads and those of the world around us. We're promised that the God of peace will soon crush Satan under our feet.[10]

If ugly memories are following you, hissing shame, as my stalker did to me, know you have been given power through the blood of Christ to turn, confront, and defeat the enemy.

Love is stronger still. It always has been.

Points of Connection

1. If you are alone as you read this, you may want to name your shame aloud. What past events cause painful memories to resurface? Consider scheduling an appointment with a trusted spiritual advisor or an experienced counselor. What steps can you take today toward the freedom that God desires for you?

2. Today's theme is grounded in Scripture. Look at several of the passages referenced, including 1 Corinthians 15:25, Romans 8:1, and Romans 16:20. As you pray these truths into your life, rest in the finished work of Christ. He has given you the authority to rise above shame. Consider adopting Psalm 34:5 as your warrior cry: "Those who look to him are radiant; their faces are never covered with shame."

Shame does not come from God. In Christ, the bonds that tied you to past pain have been broken. Walk in freedom.

HOLDING PEACE

*[Moses said,] "The L*ORD *will fight for you, and you shall hold your peace."*

WHEN MY HUSBAND AND I RELOCATED to the foothills of the Great Smoky Mountains, we named our new home Peace Ridge. The name is not only descriptive, capturing the tranquility of the long-range view, but also prescriptive. We want our home to be a place of peace and refuge for family and friends, strangers and sojourners, the weary and the wounded.

Like many properties in the mountains, ours has a small stream running down the slope. It bubbles up on one side of our drive-way and disappears underground, only to emerge again closer to the pond. I'm delighted with our tranquil water feature when it behaves. But when heavy rains cause it to flood or our lawn mower veers too close and has to be towed out, things get messy.

Just like me. I prefer my life to flow along tidily, all cares conveniently out of sight. But they're never out of mind. At inconvenient times, they flood to the surface and overflow their neatly managed little banks. I joke about being a frequent crier and scoring points for future travel, but there's nothing funny about dealing with anxiety. Again.

God's people knew something about that.

When the ancient Israelites were fleeing the Egyptians in the account of the Exodus, they panicked when they saw Pharaoh's armies closing in. As they cried out to the Lord, Moses reminded them: "Don't be afraid. Just stand still and watch the Lord rescue you today. The Egyptians you see today will never be seen again. The Lord himself will fight for you. Just stay calm."[1]

Another translation puts it this way: "The Lord will fight for you, and you shall hold your peace."[2]

Holding your peace. Isn't that just for wedding ceremonies, as in "Speak now or forever . . ."? Are we simply to keep silent, not speak unless spoken to, just shut up already and let God handle it?

Or could this promise point to something deeper?

The other day, I was feeling super anxious (deep breath, true confession) over writing this book. Who am I to have anything creatively orthodox to say about the spiritual life that has not been articulated already by writers far smarter, more educated, and more saintly than I am? If I stumble on biblical insights that truly are original, what if they're heresy?

Do you have moments like this, too, when you assume everyone else is a better parent/employee/student than you are? When your little stream of contentment dives underground, only to rage to the surface and rearrange the banks of your carefully constructed life?

When my fears of inadequacy boiled to the surface, I texted my cousin Jan, one of thirteen women laboring in prayer with me over this book, my spiritual midwives.

Jan called immediately from Texas, prayed fervently, and led me through a lengthy time of intercession and release. As she concluded our impromptu prayer meeting, Jan reminded me of the promise that became my deliverance in a time of crisis decades ago:

"Maggie, here is the Word of God for you again today: *I will fight for you, and you shall hold your peace.*"

What if God's words to the Israelites delivered through Moses are his word to you today, as they have been to me?

Rather than remaining mute or impotent in the face of life events flooding out of control, what if we take God at his Word instead and *hold our peace*?

We hold it by recognizing that the one who created the world also created us with unique capabilities. If he has called us to a task, he will enable us to complete it.[3]

We hold it by acknowledging that the Prince of Peace is actively present in our lives. When he is in residence, we don't need to offer hospitality to unwelcome guests like fear, anxiety, and inadequacy.[4]

We hold it by accepting that God has shared many of his attributes with us—but omniscience is not one of them.

If you are doing the best you can with what you know to do, rest in his peace, friend.[5]

He holds the future, but you can hold your peace.

Points of Connection

1. Jesus often taught through parables, and likewise, word pictures can help us understand spiritual concepts otherwise difficult to grasp. Visualize holding a grudge. Describe it with a few adjectives—how a grudge might feel, look, smell. Now contrast

that with how it might look to physically hold peace in your hands.

2. When Jesus first appeared to the disciples following his resurrection, he greeted them with the words "Peace be with you!" John 20:19 tells us that the disciples were meeting behind locked doors because they were afraid of the Jewish leaders. Jesus knew their greatest need was his presence, the essence of peace itself. What is your most pressing need today? What might you be hiding from? Give God permission to enter your situation and bring you the peace of his presence (see John 14:27).

Life Line

God holds the future, and because of his presence,
you can hold your peace.

WHEN JOY ELUDES YOU

*Because of our faith, Christ has brought us into this place of
undeserved privilege where we now stand, and we confidently
and joyfully look forward to sharing God's glory.*

ROMANS 5:2, NLT

*Joy to the world, the Lord is come!
Let earth receive her King.*

ISAAC WATTS, "JOY TO THE WORLD"

THIS BELOVED CAROL BEGINS on a D note and seven words later,
descends a full octave before the music begins to rise again. But
what about when your spirit will not, cannot rise with it? Does the
elusive emotion of joy seem so beyond reach you can't imagine feeling it again any time soon?

Perhaps you are grieving the winking out of a loved one's life
or the loss of a longtime relationship. Or you're forever doing for
everyone else but are seldom done for. Maybe your smile assures
the rest of us *I'm fine, thanks for asking!*, but the shadows in your
eyes say otherwise.

Joy is a product of the Spirit, the apostle Paul says.[1] Sweet and succulent, like fruit. But joy, like fruit, doesn't sprout from spent ground. Certainly, when we feel stretched to our emotional and spiritual limits, we feel more like dry husks than sweet fruit.

Henri Nouwen once wrote, "Joy does not simply happen to us. We have to choose joy and keep choosing it every day."[2] It comforts me that a deep thinker like Nouwen can put matters so easily for people like me who are wading in the shallows. And I'm reminded of what Jesus said, that fruit emerges when we're connected to the Vine. We can produce nothing fruitful, including joy, apart from him. It all makes sense.

But still I doubt. I know how it feels to try to wrestle feelings of depression, anxiety, and discouragement to the ground, only to find them lunging at me from another direction. When I talk to those who are struggling, I'm long on empathy but short on answers. Joy is a central theme in Jesus' teachings, but how do we grasp it when his Father and ours sometimes seems so far away?

So instead, I go to him with my concerns and try to make it a conversation. And that's a consternation because most times, I talk too much and listen too little. But on this chilly mountain morning, I stand outside on the porch, hugging myself to keep warm, and once again, I'm wondering how those who are suffering can find joy.

It's pondering more than prayer, accompanied by a Smokies soundtrack: the music of the stream rushing down the eastern slope of our land into the pond. Clear and swollen with mountain snow runoff, it tilts into our property from the neighbors' pond above ours, fed by streams farther up Wolfpen Mountain. I wish I could climb high enough to locate the source.

This morning, I'm thinking about something the brilliant missionary and author Amy Carmichael once said. Amy graduated to glory before I was born but left so much of herself behind—words steeped in the Word. So I pay attention when Amy speaks because her life was hard, really hard, full of dying children and social ostracism. When the courts weren't hauling her in for challenging the system, her own colleagues were turning on her.

But despite it all—or maybe because of it?—Amy once said:

> The joy of the Lord is an unquenchable thing. It does
> not depend upon circumstances, or upon place, or upon
> health . . . or upon our being able to do what we want to
> do. It is like our river. It has its source high up among the
> mountains, and the little happenings down in the river-bed
> do not affect it.[3]

Below is where we live, friends—you and me. The happenings don't seem so little, though, do they? They tumble us over sharp edges and sharper words, grinding us like sea glass, rushing us over slippery situations until we don't know whether we can keep our heads above water, much less choose joy.

But this is what I've learned after all these years with God: The fruit of my life is not grown on the mountaintops but in the valleys. Those riverbeds full of rocks and unpredictable currents? The soil is the most fertile right alongside them, my farmer-father used to say. And that's powerful, that truth. We may have no choice but to stand in the stream and go with the flow, but nothing can pollute joy when it finds its provenance in the heart of our loving, giving God.

I can't see the origin of the stream that feeds our pond here at Peace Ridge. I expect I never will. We can buttress its banks, manage the flow, stave off erosion. But the source is high above us somewhere in these mountains, "in light inaccessible hid from our eyes."[4]

And the promise I heard today in my conversation out on the porch?

> When I see you again, you'll be full of joy, and it will be a joy no one can rob from you. You'll no longer be so full of questions.
>
> This is what I want you to do: Ask the Father for whatever is in keeping with the things I've revealed to you. Ask in my name, according to my will, and he'll most certainly give it to you. Your joy will be a river overflowing its banks![5]

This world is crazily beautiful and absurdly awful. It can rob you of your stuff and your people and sometimes your wits.

But the one whose birth we celebrate each December said it true: Joy is on its way, and nothing can stop it.

> *He comes to make His blessings flow*
> *far as the curse is found. . . .*
> *And wonders of His love,*
> *and wonders of His love,*
> *And wonders, wonders of His love![6]*

Points of Connection

1. What's the difference between happiness and joy? Is there one?

2. How can we choose to be joyful when our feelings are at odds with our will?

3. Take a few moments to consider the following passages: Psalms 5:11; 103:2; and 118:24. Does the psalmist's perspective change your own?

Life Line

We cannot generate feelings of joy out of sheer willpower, but we can stay connected to the Source of all joy.

COPING WITH CRITICISM WITHOUT GETTING BURNED

If you reject discipline, you only harm yourself;
but if you listen to correction, you grow in understanding.

PROVERBS 15:32, NLT

WHEN MY HUSBAND AND I FIRST ENTERED pastoral ministry, we brought certain assumptions with us. If we were kind to others, we expected them to respond with kindness. If we offered the benefit of the doubt in circumstances when someone's actions had a less than stellar outcome, we'd receive it too. It's how relationships between believers are supposed to work. Except when they don't.

Yes, our relationships with other Christ followers often bring beauty and encouragement. But what we tend to recall more vividly are the blistering criticisms.

I remember the older man new to our church who blamed my husband for low attendance at a special event, concluding in his letter, "You and that wife of yours will never amount to anything in ministry, and neither will your church." And the well-to-do businessman who voted against granting us a long-overdue sabbatical because we hadn't been "successful" enough when it came to growing the big *B*'s: the building, the budget, and the number of butts in the seats.

Maybe you're one of those rare people who is blessedly impervious to personal attack. More likely, though, you've experienced it too. You've absorbed verbal blows from abusive family members, snarky friends, angry customers, unhappy patients, dissatisfied clients. It hurts.

God designed his human family—the pinnacle of his creation—to care for one another. In our relationships, with all their potential for joyful connection, lies the possibility of deep emotional pain. None of us is completely immune to criticism, so how can we filter it in a redemptive way?

Choose blessing rather than bitterness. Responding in love to those who seem intent on tearing you down rather than building you up is difficult. As I've navigated contentious relationships over the years, I've realized I have three choices: become bitter and build a wall, become emotionally barren and withdraw, or consider myself blessed to occasionally suffer because of the one I serve.

The apostle Peter cautions us, "Don't repay evil for evil. Don't retaliate with insults when people insult you. Instead, pay them back with a blessing. That is what God has called you to do, and he will grant you his blessing."[1] The choice, however, is ours.

Study role models in Scripture. Moses was no stranger to others' complaints, nor was David to rebuke. Mary of Nazareth kept silent in the face of the cultural scorn and misunderstanding she must have faced. Learning to respond to adversity as they did is a potent stimulant to spiritual growth. The life of Christ himself is a case study in dealing with criticism in a godly manner.

Look beyond the fault to see the need. Sometimes our accusers go on the offensive due to deep needs in their own lives that remain unseen to us. It can help to recognize that we may be absorbing others' anger that has nothing to do with us.

Contextualize the criticism. When Mike and I carefully considered the painful letter we received, we realized the writer's distance from our church situation supplied potential for misunderstanding. The businessman who opposed us was experiencing significant work-related stress. We were not the only targets of his anger. Putting ourselves in their places helped us understand them better.

Retreat to restore perspective. Think of a retreat as a strategic withdrawal. Can you get away for even a few hours to gain emotional distance from the situation? Withdrawing in order to lay your pain before God can provide the strength and insight to respond constructively.

Stop, drop, and roll. When my kids were small, this simple phrase taught them what to do if their clothes ever caught on fire. When you're blistered by criticism, you may want to apply the same advice.

- *Stop* and listen, resisting the impulse to defend yourself or withdraw. Is there something valuable you can learn?
- *Drop* to your knees and take the situation to the Father for comfort and counsel. Moses fell on his face when confronted with the Israelites' complaints and did not respond until he had received direction from the Lord.[2]

- *Roll* with the punches! Take the proactive approach. You may not be able to prevent the next verbal attack, but with God's help, you can control your response to it.

One caveat, friends. Continual, sustained verbal abuse is a different animal from the garden-variety criticism that comes with social interaction. If you're in a relationship where you're constantly subjected to demeaning personal attacks, please talk with a counselor, a trusted spiritual advisor, or your workplace HR department. If your adversary won't cease and desist, you may need to find a way out of the situation. If that's impossible at present, ask God to toughen your skin. Even that difficult strengthening process can be cause for gratitude. Underneath a tough skin, God can, in his ultimate mercy, preserve a tender heart.

Points of Connection

1. The apostle Paul, no stranger to criticism, once wrote to the Corinthians, "As for me, it matters very little how I might be evaluated by you or by any human authority" (1 Corinthians 4:3, NLT). Given how painful it is to be harshly critiqued, how could Paul write this? Read 2 Corinthians 11:16-30. What do we know about his personal history that prepared him to accept harsh criticism?

2. Irish missionary Amy Carmichael was widely celebrated for her writing and work among the people of South India, yet she was often the victim of unjust accusations and personal attack. She once wrote, "If I feel bitterly towards those who condemn me, as it seems to me, unjustly, forgetting that if they knew me

as I know myself they would condemn me much more, then I know nothing of Calvary love."[3] Perhaps you've been unfairly criticized, but are there other times you deserved rebuke for behavior that escaped notice? How can this self-knowledge provide perspective?

Burned by criticism? Stop, drop, and roll.

FINDING PEACE IN THE MIDST OF PAIN

Friends, when life gets really difficult, don't jump to the conclusion that God isn't on the job. Instead, be glad that you are in the very thick of what Christ experienced. This is a spiritual refining process, with glory just around the corner.

I PETER 4:12-13, MSG

As I sat down to type these words, a ding on my iPhone announced an incoming text. A loved one had just experienced a crushing disappointment. Again.

Three new cancer diagnoses this week among our circle of friends. A young couple whose marriage we deeply invested in just divorced. My news feed is filled with stories of natural disasters, political infighting, and social injustice.

The apostle Peter warned us. "Dear friends, don't be surprised at the fiery trials you are going through," he wrote, "as if something strange were happening to you."[1]

And yet surprised is exactly what I always am. *No, Lord, not this,* I groan. *Not him, not her, not them. Not again.*

On my first trip to Israel years ago, I looked forward to visiting the garden on the Mount of Olives, where Jesus prayed the night he was arrested.[2] *Gethsemane.* Our guide told us that the name comes from the Grecianizing of the Hebrew words *gath* and *she-men,* which mean "press" and "oil." Gethsemane was the garden of the olive-oil press, the place where the closing events of Christ's life pressed so heavily on his spirit that his sweat ran like drops of blood.[3]

I was surprised to discover that Gethsemane looked nothing like the garden I had pictured. Two thousand years had passed, of course, and the garden is now walled in to prevent visitors from breaking off branches. Yet the Church of All Nations nearby welcomes those wishing to pray. A Latin inscription above the door reads, "With many tears and supplications he makes our wants known." Visitors can kneel at the crown-shaped altar rail.

A crown of thorns. The only crown that Jesus, King of the Jews, would wear this side of eternity. The crown he was preparing to wear even as he prayed in agony in Gethsemane.

How do we endure our own Gethsemanes? How do we survive when life presses us down so fiercely that we fear we'll be crushed under its weight?

My friend Karen Mains calls these events "minor crucifixions." Karen is no stranger to suffering. She and her husband, David, were forced to close their national-broadcast ministry after a prolonged personal attack. They have dealt with debilitating illness. Most searing of all, they recently lost their youngest son to an aggressive lymphoma.

"Minor crucifixions are those passages in life when we wonder if we will possibly survive," Karen says. "They are minor in comparison to such great tragedies as the holocausts or war. And they are minor in comparison to that ultimate Crucifixion, Christ's death on the cross, in which he took upon himself the sinful calamity of the world and of history.

"[And yet] minor crucifixions, when we are enduring them, do not seem minor at all; they have the potential to make us question every belief we once held dear. But if we will allow it, they can go far in transforming us into the image of Christ."[4]

The apostle Paul was certainly no stranger to suffering.[5] In addition to everything else he had endured, he was afflicted with what he described as "a thorn in my flesh, a messenger of Satan."[6]

To those of us whose only familiarity with thorns are the kind associated with roses, this metaphor may not have the same impact as it did on Paul's first readers. "Thorn" in the Greek is *skolops*, meaning a stake or sharpened shaft that can impale the flesh. Thornbushes in the Middle East can grow to five or six feet tall, the approximate size of a human being. If you stumble into one of those in the dark, you won't emerge unscathed.[7]

Whether Paul's thorn was an illness or physical disability or adversaries who were a liability to his ministry, his focus was not on what the thorn was but on why God allowed it: in part, "to keep me from becoming conceited."[8]

So does this mean our struggles are solely intended to humble us? Why does God allow his servants to suffer so? The fuller answer comes to Paul through fervent, repeated prayer: "My grace is sufficient for you, for my power is made perfect in weakness."[9]

In the upside-down nature of God's Kingdom here on earth, the strong are made weak that we might depend on divine empowerment. To be useful, we are emptied of self, broken like the loaves and fishes that, whole, might have fed a man. But what was broken fed a multitude.

Oswald Chambers once wrote, "If you are going to be used by

God, He will take you through a multitude of experiences that are not meant for you at all; they are meant to make you useful in His hands."[10]

Are you going through a crucifixion of sorts in your own life right now that doesn't feel minor at all?

His grace is sufficient. For you. And for me.

Points of Connection

1. James, half brother to Jesus, would have been well acquainted with suffering, having witnessed the sorrows of his mother and knowing of the agonizing death his brother endured on the cross. Read James 1:2-4 (ESV). What does the apostle say is the product of the testing of our faith? How can we possibly "count it all joy"? What makes that divine arithmetic possible?

2. God redeems our suffering, but he is not the author of it. Paul describes his thorn as "a messenger of Satan," and Job's troubles were clearly of satanic origin (Job 1:6-12). The question of why God allows his people to suffer is not always answered in Scripture, but we can put our confidence in God's character as a loving Father who will give his children what we need to endure it. See Acts 3:19-20; Hebrews 10:36; 1 Peter 5:10. After God's promise to restore us, what will we become?

3. If life events have left you disappointed on many occasions, it's especially important that you find a place for hope in your daily experience. Consider 1 Corinthians 13:13 and Romans 5:3-5. How can you "be joyful in hope" (Romans 12:12) and encourage others to do the same?

Peace in the midst of pain is not just possible—it's a promise.

WHERE DO YOU GO TO GET WARM?

Be happy with those who are happy, and weep with those who weep.

ROMANS 12:15, NLT

THE PHONE RINGS, and on the other end is a longtime friend in so much emotional or physical pain she can barely speak. Your email server downloads new messages, and you read with disbelief of an accident that's befallen a family you care about. A colleague stops by your desk at work and whispers, "Will you pray for me? Things are bad at home."

How many times has this happened to you? Saying "I'm sorry" seems inadequate. Sympathy is feeling sorry for another's loss or misfortune, but God commands us to take an important step beyond pity. We are to empathize with one another.

Empathy is the God-given capacity to understand and share in the feelings of another person. Psychologists tell us that a person who lacks the ability to feel what others are experiencing is one in need of emotional help themselves. Sympathy might send a card or flowers in a gesture of genuine support, but Empathy asks, "How would I feel in her place? What must he be experiencing right now? How can I help?"

Scripture tells us that we learn to comfort others by recalling how we ourselves have been comforted.[1]

Years ago, my husband had an emergency surgery that saved his life. During the preceding nine months, though, Mike had become increasingly ill due to a mistaken diagnosis. In our despair, we appreciated prayers, calls, meals, and offers of support. What was not helpful, though, were comments that may have been well-intentioned but were ill-considered. One woman told me my husband must be sick because I didn't keep our home clean enough. Other acquaintances tried to put our situation into perspective by sharing stories of those who were worse off, as if their circumstances somehow could minimize ours.

Authors David and Nancy Guthrie, who lost two children to a rare genetic disease, remind us to give grace to those who don't know the right thing to say or do:

> When people hear about difficulty in your life, their brains search like computers for a connection. Because they don't know what else to say . . . they tend to blurt out the first "search result" that comes up: "I knew a family who had this happen . . ."
>
> It makes people feel better to suggest a resource, a solution, a book—or to tell you about someone who overcame the obstacle you face. But it doesn't always make us feel better, does it?[2]

We must be careful not to diminish someone else's pain or loss by comparison ("I know someone else who . . .") or rationalization

("Well, at least you . . ."). However well-meaning our intentions might be, it's not our place to downgrade a family's personal hurricane to a thunderstorm. Let's also be careful not to put the burden for action on their plate ("If you need anything, just call me").

The Bible points us to a different way—toward empathy. "Mourn with those who mourn," Paul wrote.[3] But how do we do that?

First, extend the ministry of presence. Maybe you can't be with your hurting friend in person, but pick up the phone or a pen. Send a text, even if the only thing you can say is, "I love you dearly, and you are not alone." Silence will deepen her pain if she's left to wonder why you're avoiding her. Research proves that visits to hospital patients from loved ones stimulate the regions of the brain that promote healing.[4] Calling or writing a suffering friend can have a similar benefit.

Second, listen and be present. Refrain from spouting Scripture. Yes, ultimately "all things work together for good,"[5] but the one who's hurting doesn't need to hear that right now. Job's so-called comforters failed when they started to lecture him. Let your friend pour out her pain. When we went through our valley, the friends who encouraged us the most were the ones who helped us face the darkness and encouraged us to persevere. We did not need their sympathy. We needed their strength.

My longtime friend Gail MacDonald offered her presence, not her pity, in the difficult months of my husband's medical battle. She later wrote this beautiful observation: "It's impressive that when Jesus was headed for the awful hours on the cross, he made no move to generate sympathy from the disciples. He *did*, however, want them close by: 'Watch with me,' and, 'Pray with me.'"[6]

If I had been nearby on that fateful night in the garden, I might have gone for a meal (stewed lamb, anyone?) or done battle with his enemies (Peter tried that). But all Jesus asked of his disciples was for them to watch and pray with him—to live out empathy by *being with* him. Can we do less for those we love?

Finally, ask God if there is more you can do to help. One of the names for the Holy Spirit is the Comforter.[7] When we listen for his instructions, God is faithful to bring to mind Spirit-led ideas for helping others that might never occur to us otherwise.

Our lives on this planet are beautifully and intricately inter-connected. God never intended his children to navigate the journey alone. When the world runs cold, we need the warmth of his presence. May others experience his love through us.

Points of Connection

1. Think back over difficult times you've experienced. What were some of the most helpful things that others said or did? How might this guide your response to others' suffering in the future?

2. Read 1 Corinthians 12:26 and Galatians 6:2. What do these passages teach us about true empathy? Now consider Hebrews 4:14-15. How does Jesus identify with us in our weaknesses?

Life Line

When times are tough and grief gnaws at your soul's edges, watch for the Comforter.

GOD WRITES STRAIGHT BY BROKEN LINES

I've learned by now to be quite content whatever my circumstances.
I'm just as happy with little as with much, with much as with little.
I've found the recipe for being happy whether full or hungry, hands
full or hands empty. Whatever I have, wherever I am, I can make
it through anything in the One who makes me who I am.

PHILIPPIANS 4:12-13, MSG

GROWING UP ON A MIDWESTERN FARM in a region known for rich soil, I used to wonder why my farmer-father made a pass through the fields before starting over again with the planter. As a child, I didn't understand the principle of cultivation: the need to break up the black loam to receive the seeds. If he didn't prepare the soil, there would be no harvest.

Ann Voskamp, writing from her family's farm in Canada, is intimately acquainted with brokenness. She relates a conversation with her husband about the need for the violent separation that's part of nature:

The seed breaks to give us the wheat. The soil breaks to give us the crop, the sky breaks to give us the rain, the wheat breaks to give us the bread. And the bread breaks to give us the feast.[1]

But what of the brokenness of human lives? The violent fractures in relationships? The separations that rip jagged lines through the portrait of a once-happy family? How can anything life-giving come from such brokenness?

The book of 2 Kings contains a visual picture of a young woman whose story is told in fewer than twenty verses.[2] We know little about her other than that she was enslaved, kidnapped from Israel and torn away from her family and all that was familiar. The dignity of her personhood was stolen when she was captured. Once a person, now she was considered property. And a position of servitude in a master's household was—then just as it is now—a precarious place for a woman.

The young woman served the wife of a man named Naaman, a commander in the military. Scripture doesn't tell us whether he was kind or brutal or if he took any notice of the slave girl. But all of that changed when Naaman became afflicted with leprosy, an incurable, contagious condition that was one of the most feared diseases of ancient times.

The young woman may have become aware of her mistress's concern, or perhaps she noticed the effects of the disease herself. It would have been natural for her to take silent satisfaction at the knowledge that the person responsible for her enslavement, the captor of the captive, was now seriously ill. She might be justified to think, *It serves him right. I hope he dies of it.*

Yet Scripture records what she did say: a handful of words that changed the course of history.

"If only my master would see the prophet who is in Samaria! He would cure him of his leprosy."

Why speak up when she'd be justified to remain silent? Why share her faith in the power of God to heal through the prophet

Elisha when this pagan leader was undeserving of mercy, let alone healing?

It's been said when you have nothing left but God, you become aware that God is enough. But enough for what?

Enough for her to let go of the bitterness that could have bound her to her captor.

Enough for her to refuse the emotional barrenness that could have resulted from the situation, an emptiness of spirit that would prevent her from having anything to give.

Enough for her to release her desire for revenge and choose forgiveness instead.

She let go of all of that and let God work. The words are so easy to say, but the burden of obedience is so very difficult.

Can you identify with her story? Perhaps you lost something precious when you were young too—a parent due to death or divorce, or a sibling or close friend who left you feeling alone and defenseless. Or perhaps you lost your own innocence through conflict you witnessed or abuse you suffered.

Is it possible to find freedom through forgiveness? To break the bonds that tie us to our past through releasing those responsible to God?

Friends from Brazil have taught me a saying in Portuguese: *Deus escreve certo por linhas tortas.* "God writes straight by broken lines." God takes the brokenness of our hearts and stories and, if we let him, uses them to write something new—to lead us into freedom.

Freedom is not natural. It is unnatural. It is supernatural.

How can we possibly forgive? Only because God first forgave us.[3]

Forgiveness doesn't mean what the abuser did was acceptable. It doesn't mean a perpetrator should not be brought to account.

God's holiness demands justice as well as mercy. We're promised one day all will be set straight.[4]

But what it *does* mean is that a captive will be set free. And that captive is you. It's me.

Forgiveness is freedom. And in your freedom, God will write straight by broken lines.

Points of Connection

1. It takes faith to believe God has a purpose and a plan in our pain. Faith is a gift from God, not something to be earned. If your faith needs strengthening (and whose doesn't?), pray through the following passages: Romans 10:17; 12:3; Hebrews 12:2.

2. What are some of the ways suffering can make us more useful in others' lives, rather than less? Read Genesis 41:52 and Hebrews 12:11.

3. Picture a cracked piece of pottery. Are there ways that what appear to be imperfections are letting in the light? How can the broken places in our lives become things of beauty in the Potter's hands?

Life Line

God specializes in creating beauty out of brokenness.

PART II

The Intentional Journey

The journey of faith, the path to spiritual wholeness, lies in our increasingly faithful response to the One whose purpose shapes our path, whose grace redeems our detours, whose power liberates us from the crippling bondages of our previous journey, and whose transforming presence meets us at each turn in our road.

M. ROBERT MULHOLLAND JR., *Invitation to a Journey*

IF I EVER WRITE A MEMOIR, I think I'll title it *The Woman Who Went Out for Pizza and Ended Up in Montana.*

Before our kids entered their teen years, Mike and I borrowed a pop-up camper and drove across the country to visit many of America's national parks with them. One evening, as it was growing dark, we pulled into a campsite next to the interstate somewhere in northern Wyoming. Mike and the kids hustled to put the camper up while I drove back to a pizza place we'd spotted on the way in. We didn't have a GPS or mobile phones in those days, but I was sure I could find my way back with our dinner.

I groaned when what I thought was the entry road to the campground turned out to be the entrance ramp for the highway instead. No big deal—I would just drive to the next exit and reverse my direction back to the campground (whose name I didn't know, in a tiny town whose name I hadn't noticed). Piece of cake (actually, make that pizza).

Only there *was* no exit. With cars whizzing by me on the dark interstate and signposts indicating that the nearest town was fifty miles away, I drove northwest for nearly an hour with stone-cold pizza in the back seat and cold-sweat panic in the front. Where in the Wild West was I, anyway? When I finally passed the "Welcome to Montana!" sign, I had a clue. Since I lived to tell the tale, you know I eventually found my family again one state back, but it sure wasn't a road trip I ever intended to make.

I bet you have a story or two like this of your own. Times when your intentions were good, but you ended up in a place you never would have chosen. Times when you meant well, but others misread your motives. Times when you went out for pizza in Wyoming and ended up in Montana.

The Irish have a blessing meant for well-intended people like us: "May you have the hindsight to know where you've been, the foresight to know where you're going, and the insight to know when you've gone too far."[1] My pastor, Chris Westmoreland, often comments that our windshield needs to be as unobstructed as our rearview mirror. Wouldn't it be lovely to see where we're going as clearly as the places where we've been?

How grateful I am—how utterly, radically grateful—that the God of our journey doesn't leave us directionless. As M. Robert Mulholland Jr. notes, God's purpose shapes our path, his power liberates us from the constraints of our past, and his transforming presence meets us at every bend in the road. The Lord sees our every intention, ill-considered or not, reveals our private motivations, and will ultimately give each one of us our due.[2]

In the nineteenth century, Cardinal H. E. Manning captured the assurance we can have in offering our lives to God:

Seeing my intentions before he beholds my failures;
Knowing my desires before he sees my faults;
Cheering me to endeavor greater things, and yet accepting the least;
Inviting my poor service, and yet above all, content with my poorer
  love.[3]

Friends, we are made with a purpose. The intentional life happens because we learn to make careful choices about the future, even as we grow in maturity from the lessons learned in the past. What God forms, he fills with his perfect will. He teaches us—through his Word and others' wisdom—to attend carefully to our daily choices. We can have confidence in our calling because the one whom God calls, he also equips.

As you thoughtfully engage with this section, I hope you'll not only learn from my mistakes but also soak in my encouragement. If, like me, you focus too often on the road trips and detours you wish you hadn't taken, please know that failure is never the final word in God's economy. If you thought you were doing it right only to have it go all wrong, that doesn't mean God wasn't present. Sometimes it's hard to see him in the windshield, but glance through the rearview mirror of your life and you'll find reminders of the times his presence was palpable.

I may have felt alone when I went out for pizza and ended up in Montana, but I wasn't. Not for a hot minute. Grace was riding in that car with me along with that cold pizza.

And it was grace that led me home. It knows the way.

FORMED AND FILLED

God created human beings in his own image. In the image of
God he created them; male and female he created them.

GENESIS 1:27, NLT

I DON'T GO ANYWHERE without an ID. My North Carolina driver's license is always in my wallet, in case I'm ever pulled over. (No plans, but you never know.) IDs are necessary for admittance to events or to pick up an online order from a store. My passport gets me through airport security for international travel. It makes sense to carry identification wherever we go.

It can be a hassle obtaining a new license when you move or a new passport if yours has expired, but you know what's absolutely, totally, radically awesome? You already carry the most important ID with you at all times.

To see how this works, let's go back to the beginning. *All-l-l* the way back to the Book of Beginnings, Genesis.[1] If you've ever wondered what role you play on planet Earth or whether your presence here makes any difference, this is the place to start.

Read the first chapter of Genesis until you come to the answer to the ultimate question of the universe: where we came from. After forming the physical world and its creatures, God produced the pinnacle of his creation: male and female humans.

Alone among God's creations, we were formed to be his image-bearers. We're created in his image, what scholars call the *imago Dei*. God's ID!

When you're carrying the Creator's DNA, you don't need to spit into a test tube and pay one of those ancestry companies to tell you where your story began. You already know.

One of my grad-school professors[2] taught that what God forms, he fills. Each location that God created, he populated. On the first day, he formed the heavens and the earth, the light and the darkness, filling them on the fourth day with sun, moon, and stars. On the second day, God formed the sea and sky, filling them on the fifth with creatures of the water and the air. Then on the third day (I love third days!), he made the earth fertile, filling it on the sixth with animals and then—the grand finale—human beings.

What God forms, he fills. What does this mean for us?

When God fills something, he assigns a function. You've got a purpose, friend. And he's got the plan.[3]

Have you considered that the location you're presently *in* is God's present *intention* for you?[4] His human family carries his divine ID, and it's the transformative task of a lifetime to grow into his image.[5] We don't represent what God looks like, but we are to mirror his divine attributes: what he *is* like.

Genesis 1 doesn't define what it means to be the *imago Dei*, but we receive clues in other contexts. Verse 27 describes our vertical relationship to God, our ID, and the remainder of the passage describes our horizontal relationship with the created order. From the beginning, our function has been to rule as God's representatives over creation. To lovingly care for it as he would himself.

And even better news? He never intended for us to do it alone, to be solitary ID carriers. "Male and female he created them." This is the beautiful complexity of community. We are to live and love together to produce successive generations of offspring, both physically and spiritually.

In the great redemptive arc of creation, the New Testament carries textual echoes of the Genesis imagery. Being fruitful and multiplying goes beyond human reproduction. We are to joyfully labor to see the Word increase and bear fruit.[6]

Because of sin, our ID became tarnished, like a dirt-encrusted mirror that loses its reflective qualities. But since Christ is the image of the invisible God, that image is restored in those who place their faith in the risen Lord.[7] It gets better and better: We become new creations!

What God forms, God fills. What God fills, he assigns a function. We don't need to guess what it might be. Jesus already told us: to love God and our fellow ID-carriers as ourselves.[8]

We live out our function in this world by loving what God loves—and God loves people.[9] All people. We get to live every day with the knowledge that we bear his image—and his *love*—in our sinews, bones, and flesh.

This fabulous legacy will outlive our lives. What will we leave behind?

Points of Connection

1. God's Word says that whatever a person thinks, "so he is" (Proverbs 23:7, NASB). What we think about ourselves affects

our lives. How have you seen this to be true in your personal walk?

2. Have paper and pen handy? Without overthinking it, jot down ten to fifteen words you'd use to describe yourself. Now look up these verses: Romans 5:1; 1 Corinthians 3:16; Ephesians 1:1; Philippians 3:20; Colossians 2:10. How do these passages describe you as a child of God? What may need to change in your thinking about who you are as God's image-bearer?

3. Pick a couple of verses from the previous question that speak to you personally. Meditate on them throughout the coming week, perhaps committing them to memory. Ask God to help you live in a manner consistent with your true ID.

Life Line

You carry God's ID in your body, spirit, and soul. Love like he loves.

THE FOCUSED LIFE

Because we know that this extraordinary day is just ahead, we pray for
you all the time—pray that our God will make you fit for what he's called
you to be, pray that he'll fill your good ideas and acts of faith with his own
energy so that it all amounts to something. If your life honors the name of
Jesus, he will honor you. Grace is behind and through all of this, our God
giving himself freely, the Master, Jesus Christ, giving himself freely.

2 THESSALONIANS 1:11–12, MSG

OUR YOUNGER SON, JORDAN, works in the tech industry and regularly upgrades his smartphone. My husband and I are happy to
receive his digital hand-me-downs. The latest device we inherited
has a portrait feature that allows amateur photographers (that
would be us) to take photos placing the subject in the foreground
while gently blurring the landscape behind. Instant focus!

Wouldn't it be great if every morning you could capture a quick
portrait of what your day should look like? The main thing you
need to accomplish, your purpose for today, would display clearly,
with every other responsibility staying in the background where it
belongs.

Let's be real. Even if you could start your day with your personal
priorities clearly established, stuff happens. You intend to write that

paper, file that report, organize the kids' clothes or your own closet. And then it's dinnertime and you're raiding the freezer for something to microwave while nothing on your list has been checked off.

I'm right there too. Often others' needs supersede my plans, or emergencies crop up. I'm usually unrealistic about how much I can accomplish in a day.

But honestly? My biggest enemy is my own two eyes wandering where they do not belong.

My attraction to digital distraction.

Maybe you've been there too. You start on a project, only to check your phone when a text comes in from a friend. It only takes a second to respond, but while the thing's in your hand, you check the weather or scroll through your Instagram feed. Then an email comes in demanding an instant response like the emergency it's not. Or your office phone rings and you think, *Why not answer now and not have to call them back later?*

There's plenty of advice (online, ironically) on how to use technology without it using you. Remove social-media apps from your phone. Track your tech time. Respond to emails and check your news feed once daily and turn off alerts. Recognize what psychologists label the "optimism bias" that makes us think we can constantly multitask without consequence.

Work from home while watching your kids? You can handle it. But driving or walking while texting? Dangerous to body as well as soul.

Ever wonder how Jesus would have conducted his public ministry if first-century Palestine had been full of digital distractions? Would he have posed for selfies with his followers or sent group texts to his disciples? Hardly.

Christ knew his mission and stated it clearly: "I have come to seek and save that which is lost."[1]

When his followers urged him to schedule his time in accordance with the demands of the crowds around him, Jesus was firm about his focus. Peter and his companions tried to compel Jesus to return to Capernaum by saying, "Everyone is looking for you!"

Jesus replied, "Let us go somewhere else—to the nearby villages—so I can preach there also. That is why I have come."[2] He wouldn't allow others to set his agenda for him.

In just three years of public ministry, Jesus accomplished all his Father put him on earth to do.

Most of us will have more years allotted to us than that, maybe even the threescore and ten spoken of in Psalms.[3] But how do we maintain our focus in a world of distractions, legitimate and otherwise? Friends, family, and coworkers have their own expectations of how we should spend our time. Do we live our own life or someone else's version?

Attend to the moment you're living right now wherever you are, whether you're preparing for your workday, caring for a child, or tackling a project. Savoring time is the best way to save it.

Do you dislike the life season you're in and wish it would pass more quickly? I've been there too. Some days I just want to close my eyes, click my heels, and wish myself out of my present state of mind.

Choose to live life with eyes wide open instead. When you're caring for that child, study her face. If you're helping someone else, remember how often you've received assistance. On that commute to work, leave the phone alone and the radio off and savor the silence.

God has equipped us to live within the peace of a focused life. Let's join him there!

Points of Connection

1. How would you evaluate your attraction to distraction? Are you generally successful in avoiding optional activities when you're working or caring for family members? If not, what strategies can you employ to make sure your priorities truly take precedence?

2. Part of the danger of continual digital distractions is the pressure social-media feeds create. It's tempting to feel we need to respond to each post, comment, or helping opportunity we see online. There will always be more needs than we can fulfill. Pastor Andy Stanley once observed, "You can't shut it all out, but you can't take it all on."[4] Ask God to make it clear when you're called to help, give, or respond—and let the rest go.

3. Reread the Scripture passage for today and note the promises there. If your life honors the name of Jesus, he will honor you. If the way you spend your time today honors him, you've accomplished all you need to. Grace is woven through the entire fabric of your day.

LifeLine

Focusing on the present allows what's truly important
to sharpen into view.

CONFIDENCE IN YOUR CALLING

The one who calls you is faithful, and he will do it.

1 THESSALONIANS 5:24

WHEN I WAS IN MY LATE THIRTIES, I was stunned to be asked to assume a major leadership role in a faith-based regional organization in New England. I had every reason to turn the position down: three young children at home, significant responsibilities at the church my husband pastored, and zero experience in fundraising.

The only thing that kept me from an immediate *no* was the tremendous respect I carried for the organization and its executive leadership. They had determined through prayer that God had chosen me, so I reluctantly agreed to pray about it.

In my deep-rooted insecurity, I felt they deserved someone far more qualified than I was. I searched the Scriptures, looking for confirmation that this call was not from God.

But as I read the stories of Moses, Jeremiah, Gideon, and Mary of Nazareth, a pattern began to emerge. None had sought a position of prominence in God's service. In fact, each one recognized his or her own inadequacy. But despite their lack of self-confidence, these servants were receptive to God's voice and ultimately responded to the promise of his presence. God himself would supply what they lacked.

Can you identify? Maybe you're a reluctant leader too, willing but cautious. Or maybe you gladly embraced God's call on your life years ago. I've had to learn that when God calls, he doesn't muffle his voice. If you're willing to be useful in his hands, you can be confident that he won't waste the gifts he's already entrusted to you.

As an example of what God supplies to those he chooses to be leaders, read the story of Saul's anointing as Israel's first king.[1] Working through the prophet Samuel, God anointed Saul, empowered him by the Spirit, and granted the authority he would need. He also provided "valiant men" to go with Saul, others whose hearts God had touched.

What more did Saul need to succeed? What more do *we* need than to know God is with us and has promised to equip us to carry out what he's called us to do?

Calling is ultimately about following, not leading. If you know when you turn in at night that you walked with Jesus, even if you accomplished nothing else, it's not been a wasted day.

Confidence in our calling is based on our identity in Christ. When we know who we are in him, we can be secure whatever our activity level, wherever we find ourselves, however our efforts appear to others. Calling is not about accomplishments, status, and titles but about remaining in relationship with the one we serve.

Great leaders know this. I once was asked to introduce Jill Briscoe, a nationally known speaker, at a large conference. In the first session, I enthusiastically recited Jill's résumé, including the titles of most of the forty-plus books she's written. As I sat down, she reached over and patted my hand. "That was very well, dear," she murmured, "but next time you can simply say, 'And here is Mrs. Briscoe.'"

You might be an emerging leader, an established one, or—like me—one with fewer years of service remaining than the ones already spent. But whatever season of life you're in, God will not leave you without significant work to do. No one else is qualified to live your life's calling.

Max Lucado writes,

> Complete with summers and songs and gray skies and tears, you have a life. Didn't request one, but you have one. A first day. A final day. And a few thousand in between. . . . You've been given *your* life. No one else has your version. You'll never bump into yourself on the sidewalk. You'll never meet anyone who has your exact blend of lineage, loves, and longings. . . . You're not a jacket in the attic that can be recycled after you are gone.[2]

Are you feeling inadequate about the responsibilities you're carrying? Feeling unequal to the tasks you've been given? Me too. (Even now, on the shady side of sixty-five.)

Our confidence must never be in ourselves. It can't be, because we'll blow it time and time again. But what God has declared good is good enough for the work he has called you to.[3]

That position I was offered decades ago? Honestly, I wasn't happy about it at first. There was nothing in it I wanted or thought I needed. I said so to God.

But you know what? I accepted the position, and it changed

the course of the rest of my life. I would have missed rich years of regional service and the opportunity to work with anointed fellow servants if I'd succumbed to my fears of failure and declined the responsibility. I am ever so thankful I said yes.

May you, too, have confidence in your calling that comes straight from the Father, who loves and equips you.

Points of Connection

1. What leadership responsibilities are you carrying at present that seem way above your pay grade? Maybe, like I did, you feel you only have 10 percent of the skills and resources necessary to succeed. Can you trust God to equip you with the remaining 90 percent? Read and reflect on Philippians 2:13.

2. God gave King Saul "valiant men" to help him carry out the work. Who are the people in your home, workplace, or church to whom you can delegate additional responsibilities or ask to come alongside you in the work? Ask the Holy Spirit to impress names upon your heart, and bring them before God.

LifeLine

Confidence in our calling rests in God's responsibility to equip us, not in our self-sufficiency.

YOUR LACK DOES NOT DEFINE YOU

We continue to shout our praise even when we're hemmed in with troubles,
because we know how troubles can develop passionate patience in us, and how
that patience in turn forges the tempered steel of virtue, keeping us alert for
whatever God will do next. In alert expectancy such as this, we're never left
feeling shortchanged. Quite the contrary—we can't round up enough containers
to hold everything God generously pours into our lives through the Holy Spirit!

ROMANS 5:3-5, MSG

I'VE BEEN THINKING OF A WOMAN I've come to know. Her marriage
ended, and she's raising her children in a challenging cultural context as a single mom. There's no work available, and even if there
were, who would watch the littles? Her meager savings have long
since run out, and the local government offers no safety net for
impoverished families.

If you've visited the pages of the Old Testament, you might
know her too. We're not given her name, but seven verses in the
fourth chapter of 2 Kings tell her story. Her husband, a pupil of the
prophet Elisha, is gone, but his debts are not. Under Mosaic law,[1]
creditors could place the debtor and his children into slavery to
work off the debt.

What would you do if someone threatened to repossess your kids? To foreclose on your family?

Scripture tells us this mom did the only thing she could. She cried out to God through his servant Elisha.[2] Maybe she howled or pounded her fists into the cold stone walls. But what God heard was an honest admission of need. No sanctimony. No faking fine. No stuffing it down.

Instead she spat it out, pouring out her pain like water from a pitcher.[3]

God's response—delivered through the mouth of his prophet— is unexpected. He doesn't ask what she's missing. He wants to know what she *has* instead.

You come to me sobbing, sister, and I'm gonna empty my wallet or start a GoFundMe campaign. But God? He's not interested in a temporary fix—he's looking for a permanent transformation. He's going to work with the little she has, not the lot she lacks.

So tell me, friend, what do you have in your house today? What are you holding in your hands?

When Yahweh put that question to Moses, the response could not have been less impressive: a stick.[4] At least the widow had a little oil, but the most the mighty leader could offer up was a worthless piece of wood.

But with that wood, God parted the waters and freed a nation. And with that oil, which stopped flowing only when the containers gathered in faith were full, God freed a family.

Since the widow was honest, I will be too. When I sit down to pour out these words to you, I've got nothing in my house either. I'm acutely aware of what I lack to produce anything fit for spiritual consumption.

Yet God's words to his daughter come to me as well. And to

you. He doesn't ask us to list what we lack, but rather to offer what we have *in* our hands for him to use.

A little bit of time? He can give you more. An abundance, in fact.

A fair measure of health? If you can't get out today, you can still pray. An aching world needs those prayers.

A painful experience you've survived? He'll use that, too, to bring someone else through.

Maybe you've done the math of your life and all you see is division and subtraction, fractured relationships and lost opportunities. But God is the master of multiplication. You see what you lack; he works with what you have. What we surrender, he reproduces: time, energy, material resources.

The widow with a little oil cried out to God, carried out his instructions, and found out how abundantly he would provide. She asked only for enough to pay her creditors, but God gave her enough to live on, as well. Too often, we plead with God and then fail to follow through on what he asks us to do.

What does your present experience make possible? How can you take this hard thing in your hands and allow God to make something beautiful of it?

The power is not in the prayer (the "crying out") or the pray-*er* (the one crying out) but in the one who hears us.[5] Faith and action go hand in hand, ours in his. The widow didn't use what she had received through God's provision without first asking directions to handle what she had been given.

Maybe today you're looking through the foreground of your frustration, seeing only what you lack. I'm praying for you to gain the long-range view of how God intends to use all you have to offer him instead.

It just might be your story we're telling one day.

Points of Connection

1. Read Deuteronomy 32:10-14 aloud. What actions does God take in this passage? List the metaphors used to describe God's redemptive work. Now put yourself in the place of the one God found in the wilderness. How do you see his activity in your life, even amid the challenges you face?

2. Offer God your "empty jars" right now. What do you have that he can use?

View your life through the lens of what you have,
not what you lack.

STEPPING IN, STOOPING DOWN, LIFTING UP

You must be compassionate, just as your Father is compassionate.

LUKE 6:36, NLT

MY FRIEND STEVE AND HIS WIFE were sitting at their kitchen table one day when their fifteen-month-old son, Isaac, toddled over. Steve noticed something under the baby's tongue and was horrified to discover a jagged piece of glass they had missed when a large bowl shattered a few days earlier. Thankfully, Steve snatched it from the baby's mouth before Isaac was injured. Steve reflected on the experience later:

> When something shatters, the broken pieces find their way into hidden cracks and crevices. Then they end up inside of us, causing pain, especially to the most vulnerable. It's easy to walk past the fragments of brokenness. We're busy and overwhelmed. And maybe that particular piece of jagged glass hasn't hurt *you*. But it is hurting *someone*.[1]

Have you ever found yourself intentionally avoiding news media in any form because of the constant flood of bad news? Hurricanes batter one coast while wildfires decimate the other. Racial tensions boil over; political divides continue to deepen in the United States and around the world. Headlines feature salacious murder stories and death in all its permutations because journalists are taught to "let blood lead." Sometimes it's all just too much. We experience compassion fatigue,[2] overwhelmed by the sheer volume of broken-ness on a global scale. We walk on by. It's not hurting us personally.

But it's hurting someone.

Jesus' parable of the Good Samaritan[3] shows us another way: the way of compassion. A Jewish man traveling from Jerusalem to Jericho was attacked by thieves who stripped him and left him for dead beside the road. A clergyman noticed the victim but chose to avoid him. An assistant in the Temple likewise passed him by. But a Samaritan, a member of a racial group despised by most Jews, felt compassion and ministered to the man's wounds and paid for his future care.

Jesus' point was clear. The one who demonstrated mercy was the one who saw need before nationality. The compassionate indi-vidual was the one who refused to step around a desperate situation but rather stepped right into it.

Scripture contains many examples of compassionate service to others. Pharaoh's daughter took pity on a Hebrew baby who seemed to have been abandoned in the bulrushes and brought him into the palace to raise as her own.[4] Certain leaders in Israel pro-vided clothes and sandals, food, drink, and healing balms to those taken captive in battle and returned them to their countrymen.[5] The native people on an island where Paul and his companions were shipwrecked showed the men "unusual kindness."[6]

On his acclaimed show that ran on public television for decades,[7] Fred Rogers became famous for inviting his viewers to be his neighbors. Many of us want to view the world as our extended neighborhood. But when our days are already packed with commitments to our own families, employers, teachers, and others, where do we find the time to genuinely make a difference?

I have a habit of promising myself that when things slow down, I'll get caught up. But they don't, and I won't. I'll never have enough time to address all the needs that concern me. I don't have the financial resources to contribute to every cause I'd like to support. There are so many, I'm tempted daily to avert my eyes, to toss the letters with the donation requests, to walk on by.

But like others before me, I've learned that compassion can help me make a difference, even to just a few. I can't care for all the world's children, but we were able to open our home to two teens who needed a family for five critical years. I can't feed the world's hungry, but I can pack meals for an international ministry in the evening after work, or make breakfast at a homeless shelter on Christmas, when young parents need to be home with their children.

Is this enough? No, it will never be. But is it something to someone? Yes.

As the Lord has continually shown compassion to his children, he will empower us to do the same.

Points of Connection

1. Have you ever experienced compassion fatigue? Sometimes we exhaust ourselves unnecessarily by overinvolvement in outside ministries God has not called us to. At other times, we may need

to be the ones to step up. What factors help you discern whether a need constitutes a call?

2. Psalm 72:12-14 is a beautiful description of the compassion God demonstrates to his people. Read this passage aloud and take time to consider each phrase. How might this serve as a model for social action in your own life?

3. Sometimes our personal life experiences prepare us to serve others with an unusual degree of empathy. If you've suffered loss, had an unplanned pregnancy, or been abused by those who should have cared for you, you may come to a place in your own healing process where you realize you have a real gift to offer others in the same situation. Consider the promise in 2 Corinthians 1:3-4: God equips us to comfort others even as he has comforted us.

LifeLine

Instead of stepping around the next need you come across, intentionally step into it.

FAST FOOD AND THE THEOLOGY OF WAITING

I've kept my feet on the ground,
I've cultivated a quiet heart.
Like a baby content in its mother's arms,
my soul is a baby content.
Wait, Israel, for GOD. Wait with hope.
Hope now; hope always!

PSALM 131:2-3, MSG

WHILE MICROWAVING MY LUNCH at work one day, I read the back cover of the frozen-food packaging. (You know you hate wasting time when you stoop to that.) But rather than a bland recitation of the virtues of their product, the marketers delivered nutritional information in three points that caught my attention: "Good Question," "Good to Know," and "Good to Remember." Which, if you think about it, is a good way to approach a lot in life.

Good Question: Why am I so impatient while waiting for anything, including the three minutes it takes to use a microwave?

Answer: Because I hate waiting. Maybe you do too. Waiting for silly things like a pot to boil or a stoplight to change. Significant things such as a job offer to materialize or a house to sell. Serious things like a medical solution to chronic pain or the return of a prodigal child.

Waiting is one of the most challenging things we do in life. It's one thing to turn the pages of a nine-month pregnancy or count down the days till a wedding when joy awaits you at the end. But waiting for the solution to that which has no promised resolution can fray the edges of your soul.

I'm convinced we need to develop a theology of waiting.

Good to Know: We're not alone in the waiting room of life. The pages of the Bible are full of stories of those who wait.

Hannah waiting for a child.

Job waiting for an end to his afflictions.

Abraham awaiting the fulfillment of God's covenantal promises.

"Be still before the LORD and wait patiently for him," wrote the psalmist.[1] "Sit still, my daughter, until thou know how the matter will fall," Naomi advised Ruth.[2]

Good to Remember: We have a choice as we wait.

One of my favorite travel advisories for this life's journey we share is found in Romans: "Be joyful in hope, patient in affliction, faithful in prayer."[3] In the light of our dilemmas, we can wait anxiously and impatiently, *or* we can wait hopefully and expectantly, knowing God has not forgotten us. His arms are not too short to reach into our present situation. His silence does not equal his absence.

"If we hope for what we do not yet have, we wait for it patiently."[4]

To wait patiently is to persevere. Our English word *perseverance* comes from the Greek words *hypó* (under) and *ménō* (remain).[5] To persevere is to remain under pressure yet keep our eyes lifted above our present circumstances.

Like you, I have a lengthy list of friends and family who are enduring difficult waits right now—release from searing pain, resolution to marital impasse, response from anonymous bureaucrats. I can often do nothing for them but come alongside on the journey, soul pressed to soul, remaining joyful in hope and faithful in prayer on their behalf.

The day is not yet over; the answer they're awaiting may yet arrive. Tolkien reminds us, "Still round the corner there may wait / A new road or a secret gate."[6]

God's at work in the wait.

Points of Connection

1. Think about something you're waiting for in your life right now. On the continuum below, where would you place your feelings as you wait? Are they closer to anxious apprehension or excited anticipation?

Apprehension   Anticipation

2. In your experience with God, do you struggle most when you don't see him at work, or when you fear he might not grant what you're waiting for? Check out Proverbs 3:5-6; Psalm 34:4-5; 1 Peter 5:7; and Isaiah 26:3-4. How do these passages encourage us to trust God when we're in a holding pattern?

3. Consider others you know and that for which they're waiting. What are some of the things in which people tend to place their hope?

4. Think back to a time when you were in the "waiting room" of life. In what ways was your faith strengthened?

Life Line

Sometimes what we wait for is not as eternally significant as what God wants to do in us as we wait.

WHEN YOU THOUGHT YOU WERE DOING IT RIGHT

GOD proves to be good to the man who passionately waits,
to the woman who diligently seeks.
It's a good thing to quietly hope,
quietly hope for help from GOD.
It's a good thing when you're young
to stick it out through the hard times.

LAMENTATIONS 3:25-27, MSG

MAYBE YOU CAN THINK OF A FEW choice words to describe what you're going through right now. I'd call it out for you, but there's a limit to how colorful we can be in a book like this.

I expect you did the best you could with what you knew to do at the time. Didn't a wise woman once say if we'd known better, we'd have *done* better?[1]

But you didn't, so you couldn't, and I hate to see you hurting over what could not be helped. One attribute our Creator chose not to share with us is that of being omniscient. He is. We're not.

You took that job in good faith, only to find out the company didn't keep faith with you.

That house that should have sold three times over is still sitting there, wolfing down your savings like it's on some kind of green-paper diet.

And then there's the guy you married who left you for someone whose name burns your lips. The infidelity, the drained bank account, the lies? You loved him once and he loved you, too, but then your marriage got knocked out by something you never saw coming.

Here's what's hardest of all: It wasn't supposed to work out this way. You saw that promise emblazoned on a thousand plaques about *knowing the plans he has for you, prospering you,* and *not harming you. Giving you hope and a future.*[2]

So if you tried to do everything right and it turned out all wrong, it couldn't be God's fault, right? Must be yours. Maybe you missed a turn or didn't read the directions right or something. If we're traveling the road in the middle of his will, things *should* go smoothly.

And yet.

I've been thinking about a certain young couple. You likely know their story too. She got pregnant; he honored his commitment to marry her. The government ordered them to go home to register; it was hot and hard and a terribly long trip, but they obeyed. At least they had God on their side. Maybe even a bit closer than that.

It wasn't poor planning or a failure to call ahead (*they* were the ones who'd been called). But when they arrived, him dusty and exhausted and her nine months prego and ready to pop, what's up with this? Nowhere to stay and no one to take them in, and this in their ancestral home with kinfolk crawling all over the place, for cryin' out loud!

Because maybe that's what Mary did. Cry. Just because she

and Joseph had done everything right didn't mean things didn't go wrong.

Or did it?

Having your first kid born in a cave[3] with nowhere to lay him but a trough meant for feeding the cows was inconvenient and uncomfortable. Truth be told, I'd have let it be known exactly what I thought of the situation.

But the young couple trusted the one who had led them there. Could it be that the place planned for them on arrival was a different sort of destination all along? Circumstances sure weren't what they expected, but that didn't mean they had wandered out of the will of their Father.

A wise man said it straight: *"God's primary will for your life is not the circumstances you inhabit; it's the person you become."*[4]

Somehow that cow trough was meant to have a place in history.

Someway that young couple was learning to lean into the arms of the one who would sustain them through far tougher times.

Sometimes bad times come to us all, no matter how straight our gate or narrow our path. You're suffering over what's been done to you, friend, or what hasn't happened yet that would set your world to rights.

But it doesn't mean you've strayed from his will. Could be you're right there on his pathway, and he never takes his eyes off you.[5]

Points of Connection

1. There are few things that feel more unjust than having entered a situation with the best of intentions, only to have it totally veer off course. You did the best you could, so why hasn't your best been good enough? Reflect on these words: "If

it is possible, as far as it depends on you, live at peace with everyone" (Romans 12:18). Why did the apostle Paul include these qualifying phrases? How does that encourage you in what you're walking through?

2. Given the many factors in your situation, which ones might look different given enough time or the supply of outside resources? Which ones, barring a miracle, will never change? Ask God for the strength to accept what you cannot change and the resilience to quietly wait for the changes you long to see.

When you thought you were doing it right and it turned out wrong, ask God to turn your good intentions into his intentions.

FEELING LIKE A PHONY

But you are the ones chosen by God, chosen for the high calling of priestly
work, chosen to be a holy people, God's instruments to do his work and
speak out for him, to tell others of the night-and-day difference he made
for you—from nothing to something, from rejected to accepted.

I PETER 2:9-10, MSG

YOU'RE A STUDENT MAKING HIGH GRADES, and yet you don't *feel* smart. You worked hard for those marks. You didn't get them because you think you're innately intelligent.

Those kids you're trying to raise? They're well fed and decently dressed, but you still believe almost any other mom could do a better job than you are. The proof's in all those pictures on social media, showing other women rocking motherhood.

When you're introduced by your business title and asked to address a conference, you smile and pretend you're confident. The truth is something else; you feel like you're faking it. It must have been luck and good timing that landed you that position in the first place.

If you've ever felt like an impostor, believing your achievements are based on factors that have nothing to do with your competence, you're not alone. Highly successful women like Sheryl Sandberg, the COO of Facebook, admit they've struggled with this too.

"Every time I was called on in class, I was sure that I was about to embarrass myself," she writes. "Every time I took a test, I was sure that it had gone badly. And every time I didn't embarrass myself—or even excelled—I believed that I had fooled everyone yet again. One day soon, the jig would be up."[1]

I'm about to tell you something that even my best friends don't know. I graduated in the top one percent of my class in high school, magna cum laude in college, and with nearly a 4.0 in grad school, but I never *ever* felt as smart as the rest of my classmates. Still don't.

My parents loved and affirmed me. No one was to blame for my spectacularly low self-esteem. I've been happily married for over forty years, but I still wince to recall how I broke off my dating relationship with Mike not once but twice because I didn't think I deserved him. (If he was as great as I thought he was, couldn't he do better than someone like me? Something must be wrong with him.)

No, something was wrong with me. The Impostor Syndrome.

This phenomenon was identified early in my working career,[2] but I didn't become aware of it until recently. It doesn't mean those who struggle with it are actual fakes or frauds. Instead, we believe our success is a mistake or maybe the result of some "undeserved good fortune."[3]

Sandberg says these feelings are symptomatic of a bigger problem: "We consistently underestimate ourselves. Multiple studies in multiple industries show that women often judge their own performance as worse than it actually is, while men judge their own performance as better than it actually is."[4]

So how do we push back against impostor syndrome? Is it time for some kind of Christian feminine manifesto boldly declaring to the world that we're smart, deserving, and capable of greater things than we can imagine?

We already have it.

Scripture repeatedly affirms our worth and value in God's eyes. We are his beloved daughters.[5] We are completely accepted and fully whole.[6] We're not enslaved to insecurity but confident bearers of God's own image.[7] We are his masterpiece,[8] a real piece of work in the most glorious sense.

The key to living authentically is not finding creative ways to boost our self-confidence. Those "I'm worth it" ads are eye-rollers for me. My friends will tell you I have no more self-confidence than I did when I was a middle schooler.

What has literally changed my life is God-confidence. My life-long insecurity could have crippled me, and sometimes I still walk with an emotional limp.[9] But I can testify to the power of a loving Creator who empowers all of us to do the work he's prepared in advance for us to do.

I have a sign (with thirty-four-point font) posted over my desk that's my warrior cry: "The one who calls you is faithful, *and he will do it.*"[10]

We're Designer Originals, friends—each messy, insecure, beautifully imperfect one of us. Not an impostor in the bunch.

Points of Connection

1. In what areas of your life have you wrestled with feeling your accomplishments have been undeserved—products of luck or of being in the right place at the right time? Where might these feelings come from?

2. Take time to read the Scripture references for this reading aloud (Genesis 1:27; John 1:12; Romans 6:6; Romans 15:7; Ephesians 1:5; Ephesians 2:10; Colossians 2:9-10; 1 Thessalonians 5:24; 1 Peter 2:9-10). What do these tell you about your true identity in Christ?

3. What's one step you can take this week to declare your independence from the impostor syndrome? Offer your desire to live freely and authentically to God and ask him for the confidence only he can give.

Life Line

You are not a fake or a fraud. You're a Designer Original.

ON BEING SECOND

[Jesus said,] "When you're invited to dinner, go and sit at the last place. Then when the host comes he may very well say, 'Friend, come up to the front.' That will give the dinner guests something to talk about! What I'm saying is, If you walk around all high and mighty, you're going to end up flat on your face. But if you're content to be simply yourself, you will become more than yourself."

LUKE 14:10-11, MSG

HAVE YOU EVER BEEN DISAPPOINTED, even devastated, for coming in second when you were so hopeful that the top spot would be yours?

Sports announcers covering the Olympics have commented that it's brutal to come in second. When you're the winner, you're golden. To get the silver means you still get to ascend the podium. But to have come so close to taking first only to lose to someone else is tough. You force a smile and choke out your congratulations, but inside you're swallowing bitter disappointment.

Most of us will never compete as professional athletes, but we'll serve in subordinate roles under others who've been awarded positions we may have aspired to. We need to learn to follow well when many times, we'd prefer to lead. As one pastor put it, we need to leverage influence even when we lack authority.[1]

Barnabas knew something about being second. We may remember Barnabas by his nickname, Son of Encouragement,[2] but we often forget that he may actually have been the leader[3] on what's typically referred to as Paul's first missionary journey, which began on the island of Cyprus, Barnabas's home.[4] Barnabas was the one who introduced Paul to the circle of apostles, defending him in the face of skepticism about Paul's preconversion reputation as a murderous zealot.[5]

Yet as their ministry partnership progressed, it was Paul who took the lead. Paul, who's remembered as the great apostle to the Gentiles. Barnabas remained supportive of him until a significant conflict arose, leading to "sharp disagreement"[6] and a separation of ways. It happens. It's not easy being second.

But it's vitally important.

In our first pastorate, an older man who had served the church in an interim capacity during the pastoral search continued to attend after we arrived. Reverend Allen[7] was short on encouragement and long on criticism. It had to be difficult for him to have his authority diminished when the new pastor arrived. His subsequent behavior certainly made it difficult for us.

In our second church, however, we experienced the exact opposite. The interim pastor and his wife continued to attend but could not have been warmer or more welcoming. Dr. Quicke had moved from the pulpit to the pew but consistently referred pastoral matters to my husband. The two became fast friends.

Beautiful music results when a skilled musician plays that second fiddle well.

So, exactly how do you relinquish authority? What's necessary when submitting to someone else's leadership? How do you play harmony when someone else is calling the tune?

It helps to remember two things.

First, *humility*. (Oh gosh, you knew this was coming. But wait, it gets better.)

We mustn't mistake humility with weakness or subservience. Humility finds its origin in the Latin *humilis*, meaning "low" or "from the earth" (humus). Humus is rich, fertile soil for producing crops, useful to those for whom they're being farmed.[8] Scripture commends humility as a foundational virtue, telling us that fear of the Lord teaches wisdom, and humility precedes honor.[9] We're to be responsive to and respectful of those who are leading us. What's the point in making things harder for them?[10]

In my first full-time position after college, I replaced an administrator who was retiring, inheriting his staff in the process. They had every reason to resent having an inexperienced twenty-two-year-old supervisor. I had every reason to be terrified. I desperately needed their help and guidance, and after an initial period of adjustment, they graciously provided it. Humility was the grace-agent that moved us all forward.

Second, *we shouldn't confuse humility with low self-esteem*. The first is biblical; the second is not. I have struggled my entire life with an automatic assumption that just about anyone can do just about anything better than I can. But healthy self-esteem is not thinking less of ourselves, but rather thinking of ourselves less.[11] Being useful in God's Kingdom is not about lifting ourselves up or putting ourselves down. Let God be in charge of that particular elevator.[12]

Maybe you've been called to serve in a subordinate role, or someone else is now in a position of leadership and influence you once enjoyed. Resolve to support them fully without bitterness, using the unique skills you possess to strengthen your team or organization.

Let the Holy Spirit call the tune, and play that second fiddle well.

Points of Connection

1. Where are you right now? Are you in a position of leadership, or are you playing second fiddle to someone else calling the tune? You might be in both places in different areas of your life. How can humility help the situation, whether you're leading or following?

2. Read Hebrews 12:11, Hebrews 13:17, and Proverbs 15:33. How do you sense the Holy Spirit is speaking to you?

3. In what ways is genuine humility distinct from low self-esteem? What do you think Paul meant when he wrote about the nature of true apostleship (leading for Christ) in 1 Corinthians 4:1-13?

Life Line

Beautiful music results when a skilled musician plays
second fiddle well.

WHAT I SAW AT THE GYM ON MULBERRY STREET

*Friends, I'd say you'll do best by filling your minds and meditating
on things true, noble, reputable, authentic, compelling, gracious—the
best, not the worst; the beautiful, not the ugly; things to praise, not
things to curse. Put into practice what you learned from me, what you
heard and saw and realized. Do that, and God, who makes everything
work together, will work you into his most excellent harmonies.*

PHILIPPIANS 4:8-9, MSG

ALL RIGHT, IT WASN'T *really* on Mulberry Street, but I'll leave the
gym's exact location unspecified to protect the guilty. You see, some
of my fellow gym rats sported apparel that I deemed disastrous.
Call it felonious fashion or what not to wear. I was self-conscious
about how I looked in my workout clothes, but maybe compared
to others I didn't look quite so bad.

There was the older man on the treadmill right in front of me,
perspiration gleaming off his balding head, big yellow shirt pulled
down over shorts too tiny for the terrain they were intended to
cover. Hot pants for the geriatric set.

On my far right was a tall, thin, red-faced young mom wearing a white T-shirt soaked with sweat. As she spun and turned, I had the odd sensation of watching a human barber pole in motion.

To my left was an unsmiling teenage girl on a stationary bike. As her thick brown ponytail swung aside, I could see a single word emblazoned on her baggy blue T-shirt: "Whatever."

Whatever. The ultimate expression of postmodern tolerance. A word smacking of jaded cynicism and bored dismissal. I-don't-care-and-you-can't-make-me. Maybe it summed up the total life philosophy of this fifteen-year-old.

Or maybe not. When her ponytail swung the other way, I saw the rest of the words on the back of her shirt.

Whatever. **Philippians 4:8.**

Come again? This is one of my favorite Scripture verses: the apostle Paul's reminder to the people of Philippi to watch what they were thinking about.

Whatever is true, whatever is noble, whatever is right, whatever is pure, whatever is lovely, whatever is admirable—if anything is excellent or praiseworthy—think about such things.[1]

BUSTED. While I was trying to discipline my body, my mind had been running amok. Out of my own insecurity over the twenty extra pounds tucked into my workout clothes, I had been evaluating the way others looked too. And it took two words on a teenager's T-shirt to convict me.

Whatever is **true**, whatever is **noble**, whatever is **right**, whatever is **pure**, whatever is **lovely**, whatever is

admirable—if anything is **excellent** or **praiseworthy**—
think about such things.[2]

Have you ever found yourself regarding other people critically
without even realizing you're doing it? Psychologists tell us that we
sometimes project negative perceptions on others because of how
we feel about ourselves. We see the world not as it is but as we are,
or as we want it to be.

That older man with the too-small shorts? He was working out
at the gym rather than relaxing in front of his TV. The young mom
sweating while she spinned? She was taking time to care well for
herself in the midst of the craziness of caring for young children.
The teenager who sported Scripture on her shirt without worrying
what others might think? I admired her courage.

The apostle Paul, well aware of his own past, gave excellent
counsel to the church at Philippi: "Friends, I'd say you'll do best by
filling your minds and meditating on things true, noble, reputable,
authentic, compelling, gracious—the best, not the worst; the beautiful, not the ugly; things to praise, not things to curse."

Whatever is true, noble and right, pure, lovely and admirable?
Anything that's excellent or praiseworthy? Look for the good in
others, and you'll find more of it in yourself.

So I did.

And to think that I saw it on Mulberry Street.[3]

Points of Connection

1. How about you? Do you find yourself evaluating others
    critically? Are the factors that trigger your negativity switch
    internal or external?

2. Read Philippians 2:5. What are some of the ways we can discipline our minds to reflect the attitude of Christ?

3. A beautiful old hymn contains a powerful call to action. What would it look like to live out these words in your everyday life?

> *May the mind of Christ, my Savior,*
> *live in me from day to day,*
> *by his love and pow'r controlling*
> *all I do and say.*[4]

Do you discipline your body but let your mind run wild? Having the mind of Christ changes how we view others as well as ourselves.

WHAT WE CAN'T SEE

Just then his disciples came back. They were shocked. They couldn't
believe he was talking with that kind of a woman. No one said
what they were all thinking, but their faces showed it.

JOHN 4:27, MSG

EARLY ONE MORNING IN MAY, I paused for a moment to admire
the flowering white bushes just outside the employee entrance of
my office building. Normally, I hurried through the door without
giving them a passing glance. But for ten or so glorious days each
spring, these serviceberries bursting with blooms made me take a
second look.

I waved my key card over the automatic lock and heard the tiny
click accompanying the green light that signaled the open door. As
I stepped inside and rounded the corner near the elevator, a slightly
built woman with salt-and-pepper hair smiled as she passed, then
paused and turned back toward me.

"Maggie, I've been thinking about Margie," Judy[1] said hesitantly. "How is she?"

Margie had worked in my department the past several years.

Possessed of a rare ability to track joy into every room she entered, Margie was utterly unselfconscious in a way that marks those who consistently focus on others. When an aggressive metastatic disease left her gasping with pain late that winter, Margie reluctantly resigned in order to engage the enemy full-time.

I briefly shared the latest medical update we had but was puzzled. Judy worked in a different part of the building in a department that never interacted with mine. "I didn't realize you knew her," I commented.

"Oh, I don't really," she said softly. "Margie wouldn't even know my name, but I was using the microwave in the cafeteria one day at lunchtime when she stopped and smiled at me.

"'What a pretty pink sweater you are wearing,' she said to me. 'You look so nice!' That was all."

Judy looked down at the floor for a moment. She didn't need to say it; I saw it in her face. In a world where the young and fit attract attention, Judy and women like her are invisible. Like many middle-aged women who live alone, Judy has no one to tell her she looks nice. No one to notice when she comes home late, or not at all. Perhaps no one had complimented her in a very long time.

"Tell Margie . . . ," she started, and then faltered. "Tell her— would you please?—that the woman in the pink sweater says hello." Judy's eyes brimmed with tears. "And that I am praying for her."

And she hurried off.

For fifty weeks of the year, those bushes at the entrance of my building barely attract notice. That day I had stopped to admire them simply because they were blooming.

But how much do I miss every week of the year? People who are alone, unassuming, quietly going about their day. Men and women alike with no special attributes to draw my distracted attention.

People who are invisible until someone pauses long enough to actually see them.

Whether you're in a café, your school commons, or a church pew, maybe you've felt invisible at times too. Sometimes we even draw false comfort from loneliness, assuming that if we don't attract attention to ourselves, we won't get hurt. But it aches when people fail to notice us or call us by name.

Try an experiment. The next time you feel overlooked, challenge yourself to be the one to extend your hand or an invitation. If you're an introvert like me, it won't come naturally. But you just might be surprised to discover that the one you reached out to has been feeling invisible too.

Lord, give us eyes like Margie's to pay attention and see those we usually pass by.

Points of Connection

1. Can you think of a time when you felt totally invisible? Did anyone reach out to you? If so, what difference did that interaction make in your life?

2. Sometimes others label us not good enough to merit attention from someone important, like the disciples did with the Samaritan woman in the Gospel of John. Read Luke 12:6-7. What does this passage affirm about our worth in God's sight?

3. Think about people you regularly encounter in your neighborhood, workplace, or faith community. Are there individuals you fail to notice? What is one positive step you can take this week to reach out to someone who may be feeling insignificant or overlooked?

Life Line

It's natural to want to be noticed. There's something even better than
receiving positive attention, though: paying it to others.

NO MORE FALSE FACE

To the faithful you show yourself faithful;
to those with integrity you show integrity.

PSALM 18:25, NLT

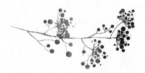

I BET IT'S HAPPENED TO YOU, TOO. You dash to the grocery store for an item featured on sale, only to find a substitute product in its shelf space. A friend who worked nights as a supermarket stocker told me it's common practice in the retail industry. If something is out of stock, employees move adjacent items over to hide the empty space, a practice called "false face." To false face is to mask the fact that something is missing.

Fakery is everywhere in contemporary culture, where social-media followings substitute for the popularity we craved in middle school. Entrepreneurs feed attention addiction by providing photo ops designed to look as if the subject is glamming it up in a tropical location or flying in a private jet that is simply a stage prop.[1]

We know what we view on social media doesn't always resemble real life. We refrain from posting photos we think make us look fat or tired or old. We don't record the moments the dog poops on the carpet or the baby projectile vomits all over the kitchen. We post #happy shots of weddings and vacations and cute kids, and you know what? That's okay. We share what we're comfortable with. If our messes are made by others, best not to broadcast them, anyway.

Where life gets wonky is when we begin to "false face" in real life: pretending to be someone we truly are not. Presenting one image to the world when a camera turned inward would capture someone quite different. Moving things around on the shelves of our lives in order to hide the fact that something vital has gone missing.

Our integrity.

Integrity is a character attribute without a dark side. A person of integrity is one who's not only honest but honorable. Down-to-earth while morally upright. Of good character even when in bad company.

A beautifully whole person.

A pastoral search committee once asked me in a phone interview how I would describe my husband, their leading candidate. I could have commented on the quality of his sermons or his love for his family. Instead, I blurted out the first thing that came to mind: "He's a man in whom there is no guile." Mike's personal integrity has always been the foundation on which my trust in him rests.

The phrase comes from the Gospel of John, in the account of Jesus calling his disciples. When Jesus saw Nathanael approaching, he knew him to be a man of integrity: "Jesus saw Nathanael coming to him, and saith of him, Behold an Israelite indeed, in whom is no guile!"[2]

To be guileless is to be an individual without deceit, innocent of any hidden agenda. The one who saw through to Nathanael's heart said of him, "Not a false bone in his body."[3]

No false face either.

Most of us would never be tempted to murder, rob, or intentionally harm another person. But integrity is tested in the small things of life: the subtle, socially acceptable little sins our culture not only allows but encourages.

The white lie. The casual gossip. The "borrowing" of office supplies. Scripture warns us of the cost of deception: "If you are faithful in little things, you will be faithful in large ones. But if you are dishonest in little things, you won't be honest with greater responsibilities."[4]

We sell our integrity for so little.

But Christ came to give us so much more. He died that we might live, not just somehow but abundantly. Exuberantly, without fear of others discovering our dark corners. Living as gloriously whole persons with no regrets.

Russian novelist Aleksandr Solzhenitsyn wrote, "You can resolve to live your life with integrity. Let your credo be this: Let the lie come into the world. Let it even triumph. But not through me."[5]

If we add to or subtract from the truth, it's no longer true. The next time I'm tempted to put on a false face or to "fake fine," I pray instead that the character God desires for each of us will show through instead.

You too?

Points of Connection

1. Read Proverbs 11:3; 19:1; and 20:7. What does this book of wisdom have to say about living as a person of authentic character?

2. The book of 2 Kings supplies several examples of Israelites who acted with integrity. See 2 Kings 5:16 and 12:15. What do you

notice about the prophet Elisha's refusal to take money, and the workmen who needed no accounting for their use of funds? Contrast that with the behavior of the priests in 2 Kings 12:4-8. What differences do you notice?

3. God does not condemn us when we make bad choices, but his Holy Spirit does work to bring us under conviction. What's the difference? For the distinction, turn to Romans 8:1, 33-34 and John 16:8.

Life Line

Integrity is doing the right thing for the right reason as we align our actions with God's character.

AGING GRATEFULLY

The godly will flourish like palm trees . . .
For they are transplanted to the LORD's own house.
They flourish in the courts of our God.
Even in old age they will still produce fruit;
they will remain vital and green.

PSALM 92:12-14, NLT

THERE'S SOMETHING ABOUT AGE that makes houses—and people
—interesting.

When I go for walks, I'm an observer. Not the creepy kind who
looks in windows, but the curious sort who loves looking at those
windows and the structures that surround them. Cookie-cutter
houses in a strictly regulated subdivision don't catch my attention,
but one-of-a-kind homes in a historic district do. The older and
more idiosyncratic, the better.

Maybe I have an affinity for anything vintage because it char-
acterizes me, too. The furniture that filled my childhood home is
now in demand as midcentury modern. High-school students discuss the sixties and seventies of my educational years as the ancient
history that it is. AARP has had my peers in their database for over
fifteen years. I am a woman, as they say, of a certain age.

And darn thankful for it.

Most of the time, anyway. No need to cite the downside of the aging process. The advertising industry reminds us daily that we should deny or defy or decry those crepey folds on our necks and the crow's-feet around our eyes. Extra pounds cling even more stubbornly in the second half of life than the first. Vintage architectural details are charming, but it's hard to say the same about the physical ones.

On a trip to the Middle East several years ago, my husband and I realized that the apostle Paul may have been close to our age when he hoofed it throughout Greece and Turkey (then Asia Minor). We traveled in an air-conditioned tour bus; Paul most likely was on foot. He must have been acutely aware of the toll his calling took on his aging body.

"Outwardly we are wasting away," he wrote to the people of ancient Corinth, "yet inwardly we are being renewed day by day."[1]

I love that perspective. So what if the structure my soul is stored in shows signs of age? It's sheltered me for nearly seven decades already. That makes it a classic!

I do what I can to maintain my soul's dwelling place. I exercise,[2] fill it with fuel, and slap paint on the exterior. But inside, where it matters most, is where personal renewal happens. Every single day we draw breath is an opportunity to rebirth our own dreams and encourage others in theirs.

I asked a diverse group of women on social media how they approach the aging process. Their wealth of positivity spanned a wide range of practical ideas, long-range goals, and spiritual perspectives.

Many women spoke of their desire to stop accumulating possessions so they can focus on the essentials. Linda is only in her fifties but is already engaged in "Swedish death cleaning"—purging her life and home of unnecessary stuff so her kids won't have to. She says, "My husband and I value time more than we ever have, and we don't want to use it maintaining a lifestyle when building into other people is so much more important."

My friend Lea has taken up painting in her retirement years, and the talent she's developed has opened up opportunities to exhibit and share her faith. "I love meeting new people," she enthuses. "My world is bigger than ever, and I'm excited about the years to come."

My former college roommate Dale has had a highly successful career as a magazine editor, author, businesswoman, and humanitarian. She and her husband study Scripture together and continue to take classes through lifelong-learning programs. They also engage in purposeful travel, visiting marginalized people groups around the world to invest their expertise in bettering others' lives.

Countless seniors stress the importance of acquiring new skills as the decades pass. Dick and Marge took up running in their late sixties, and at eighty-plus have a wall full of medals from the half-marathons they've completed. At sixty-six, Lucinda tries to learn some new technology every quarter. "It helps me get over my fear and intimidation of things I don't understand," she comments, "plus I can hold my own in conversations with my kids and high-school students!"

According to my informal online poll, the biggest plus to aging is grandchildren. Darlene said it best: "My grands are my anti-aging solution. They force me to stay fit so I can come running when they call. They turn my focus to the future and to working to improve the world they're coming into. I live to put my handprint on their lives and pass on to them the promise of their spiritual inheritance."

The one word that pops up in most conversations about aging, however, is *gratitude*. How can we bemoan getting older when so many are denied that privilege? Author Tim Kimmel has written that God extends each of us a timeline of credit, and he can exercise his option to call in the loan.[3]

Time to come clean. I've been tempted to obscure the fact that I'll be nearly sixty-seven when this book comes to print. Our Western culture values youth. I've worried that younger readers might think an older author will not be able to relate to their lives.

I'll let you be the judge of that. But you know what? I am ever so thankful you're reading these words right now. I've hammered on the door of heaven, asking God to use this book written by a woman of a certain age to build courage and confidence into your own life, whatever season you're in. I am grateful, deeply grateful, to have lived long enough to do so.

And you know what else, dear one? God has "greater things than these" for you to accomplish, as well.[4] For all the years I have left, I will be cheering you on.

I'm fond of the old homes in my neighborhood, and I'm grateful for mine.

Both of them.

Points of Connection

1. How do you feel about over-the-hill parties, greeting cards, and the plethora of jokes about older people? More importantly, how many people that you know have experienced difficulty in obtaining employment in their older years? Do you think

ageism might be the most pervasive method of discrimination in our culture? How can you be a champion and an advocate for people of every age?

2. Scripture contains many accounts of women and men in their older years who accomplished great things for God. Three siblings alone—Miriam, Aaron, and Moses—were in their eighties and nineties when they became instrumental in leading the Israelites out of bondage in Egypt. Read the following passages: Proverbs 9:11; 16:31; Isaiah 46:4. What does God have to say about how we should approach our older years? What promises does he make to us?

Life Line

Instead of denying or defending your age, embrace it. You've fought hard to get there.

PART III

The Relational Journey

God of our life,

there are days when the burdens we carry

chafe our shoulders and weigh us down;

when the road seems dreary and endless,

the skies gray and threatening;

when our lives have no music in them,

and our hearts are lonely,

and our souls have lost their courage.

Flood the path with light,

run our eyes to where

the skies are full of promise;

tune our hearts to brave music;

give us the sense of comradeship

with heroes and saints of every age;

and so quicken our spirits

that we may be able to encourage

the souls of all who journey with us

on the road of life, to your honor and glory.

ST. AUGUSTINE, QUOTED IN MAGGIE OMAN SHANNON,
Prayers for Hope and Comfort

Let's say you're on an extended trip to Europe or the Middle East. Which would you choose—visiting historical sites with a private guide or touring as part of a group? It seems like an easy choice: With an individual guide, you have the advantage of moving quickly, bypassing the larger groups massing to enter popular sites. Best of all, bathroom stops are brief! Who would want to travel any other way?

Some years ago, my husband and I received a sabbatical grant that enabled us to explore the ancient roots of the Christian faith in Turkey and Greece. With a private guide in Turkey, we went at our own pace and didn't have to consider others' needs, wants, or preferences. In Greece, however, we journeyed as a cluster of forty-two people, adjusting our pace to those who needed to move more slowly while sharing our guide's attention. As we traveled together, we processed what we were learning and experiencing together. When a member of our group needed medical attention, others quickly stepped up to offer aid. If someone received difficult news from home, the group mobilized to pray. It didn't take us long to appreciate what we had been lacking in Turkey: community. Sometimes you don't know what you've been missing till you find it.

When God declared at the outset of human history that it wasn't good for man to be alone, we see the first emergence of the beauty of community. Author David G. Benner notes that the life of the Christ follower is not a solo endeavor: "No one can make any real progress on this journey alone. Journeying together is the only way to effect the personal transformation that is the goal of the adventure."[1]

Few of us would deny the importance of family, friends, and community in our lives. It's often been said that we travel faster alone but farther together. As much as I value times of quiet and solitude, I'm grateful that life is a team hike.

Our fellow pilgrims in Greece got along splendidly, but what about other life travelers—the ones we work, play, live, or worship with? Wherever people are in close proximity for any length of time, misunderstandings, conflict, and disagreements can erupt. Loving and investing in others can set us up for deep disappointment when our investments fail to yield much of anything in return. People we've known for years suddenly bail, leaving us flailing for answers. The relationship between the first pair of siblings on the planet, Cain and Abel, ended up with one of them dead at the hands of his brother. God has always had problems with his children too.

But despite the risks inherent in all relationships, we stand to gain so much by choosing to love and live with others. Our interactions with companions on the trail are what God ultimately uses to transform us most closely into his image.

Community. Sometimes you don't know what you've been missing till you find it.

KINDRED SPIRITS

*[Jesus said,] "This is my commandment: Love each
other in the same way I have loved you."*

JOHN 15:12, NLT

Is SHE OUT THERE, you think? Your "Diana"?

One of the most poignant expressions in literature of the long-ing for a close friend comes from Lucy Maud Montgomery's classic *Anne of Green Gables.* Not long after the orphaned Anne Shirley comes to live with the Cuthberts, Anne says wistfully to Marilla, "A bosom friend—an intimate friend, you know—a really kindred spirit to whom I can confide my inmost soul. I've dreamed of meeting her all my life."[1]

When my daughter Amber was young, Anne was her favor-ite literary character. Still is. We read Montgomery's books and watched the Canadian miniseries starring Megan Follows countless times. When I flew to Tacoma to help Amber after the birth of her first child, we watched the series together again. At six, my grand-daughter already understands why we love Anne so much. At its heart, Anne's is a story about friendship.

When Anne is introduced to a neighbor girl her age, she blurts out, "Oh, Diana . . . do you think you can like me a little—enough to be my bosom friend?"[2] In her loneliness, Anne risks being vulnerable in order to make a friend. Can you relate?

As women, it's said we're wired to "tend and befriend." We're many things: CEOs and homemakers, entrepreneurs and employees, married and single. Yet at our core, we want to be cared for even as we care for others. We want to know we're not alone.

Men have a deep capacity for friendship as well, although some are slower to realize they need it. (Have you ever tried to set up a playdate for your husband?) Journalist Elliot Engel was deeply moved by the close relationship his wife had with her best friend. "Her three-hour talks with friends refresh and renew her far more than my three-mile jogs restore me," he commented in a *Newsweek* article. "In our society it seems as if you've got to have a bosom to be a buddy."[3]

We. Need. Friends.

God designed it that way. Wisdom Literature in Scripture emphasizes the need for cooperation, working together rather than jockeying to be first.[4] And while the "cord of three strands" is often taken to refer to the strengthening presence of Christ within a marriage relationship, its meaning is broader than that. It's not good for men or women to be alone, regardless of marital status. We are created for companionship.

Empathy is at the core of camaraderie. C. S. Lewis famously wrote, "Friendship is born at that moment when one person says to another, 'What! You too? I thought I was the only one.'"[5]

In a mobile society where we're continually uprooted by job transfers and other factors, where do we find that kindred spirit, bosom buddy, sister of the heart?

Let's unpack the possibilities. Some friendships begin in shared seasons of life when we're walking side by side with another in the same neighborhood or school, raising kids or building a career together. Other friendships are nurtured through shared activities or affinities when we're working side by side on a committee, sweating in a spin class, or raising funds for a community organization. Another powerful bond is shared faith: worshiping side by side, praying, or doing Bible study together.

I used to say to my kids, "Do you need a friend? Join a team." It's amazing how quickly friendships can develop when you join a musical group, sports team, or theatrical cast. When you're working toward a common goal of winning that game or acing that opening night, you bond through shared experiences.

But do you know what I've discovered is the greatest friend-finding principle of all? Simply being in the place God has for you, doing the things God has for you to do.

Jesus put it this way: "More than anything else, put God's work first and do what he wants. Then the other things will be yours as well."[6] Earlier in that same passage, he taught that we're not to worry about our lives (what we eat or drink) or about our bodies (what we wear). If God has promised to take care of those physical things, he'll bring us the friends we need as well.

"You are my friends if you do what I command," Jesus taught.[7] Obedience. Being in the place he's called us, doing the things he's called us to. When we are faithful to follow, we can trust him to meet all our needs, including the powerful need for friendship.

New England novelist Sarah Orne Jewett once wrote, "Yes'm, old friends is always best, 'less you can catch a new one that's fit to make an old one out of."[8]

I have known loneliness. Lots of it. My prayers are with you, too, that you'll soon catch some new friends fit to make old ones out of.

And until then, you've got a friend in me.

Points of Connection

1. Think of some unlikely friendships that turned out to be enriching for you. If you're reading this with a group, share some examples where you've found "sisters of the heart." (Could it be that someone in your world right now is searching for a new friend too?)

2. Women are often the best advocates for other women. If you're in a new place right now without old friends, consider joining a local advocacy group that seeks to meet the needs of marginalized or vulnerable women. How does focusing on others' needs help put your own into perspective?

3. What are some examples of women's friendships in the Bible? Check out the interactions between cousins Elizabeth and Mary in Luke 1:39-56 and mother-in-law/daughter-in-law Naomi and Ruth in the book of Ruth. List a few of the characteristics of these friendships. What qualities do you most want to develop to be a trusted friend to others?

LifeLine

If you're seeking friends, seek to be friendable.

MAGGIE'S TEN COMMANDMENTS OF FRIENDSHIP

A friend loves at all times.

PROVERBS 17:17

WHETHER YOU'RE IN YOUR YOUNGER or later years, married, single, or single again, working in the home or out of it, friendships matter. Deeply. And relationships that matter deeply can easily get messed up. Majorly.

I've been speaking about the friendships of women since the early 1990s. I know that makes me practically ancient, but the topic will never be. We don't outgrow our need for friends. My mom, who lived with us until she passed away at nearly ninety-five, came home one day glowing after a lovely luncheon with some other widows she met shortly after our move to North Carolina. When I knew Mom had new friends, I felt like a proud mama. (Oh wait, she was mine.)

Wouldn't it be fabulous if we could make friends as easily as we did when we were four, when we just grabbed the hand of the nearest girl at the playground and were instant BFFs, banded together against grubby boys with their crud and cooties? When we grew up together laughing at the same jokes and passing notes (maybe you texted) after those same boys turned out to be super cute?

But, as we all know, friendships can be full of theatrics too. High drama. And it can hurt.

Years ago, I came up with what I dubbed my Ten Commandments of Friendship. They're inspired by Scripture[1] but are clearly not Scripture themselves, so to grant them a bit more gravitas, here's the King James version:

1. **Thou shalt never put thy friendships above thy God.** Who do you turn to first when you're troubled or need direction? Do you get on the phone or go to your knees? We need to be careful not to make our friendships a higher priority than Christ's lordship. Do you expect from friends that which only Jesus can truly provide? It's a setup for disappointment. He alone is our hope.[2]

2. **Thou shalt cherish thy friend for who she is, not for who you want her to be.** Ask yourself if you ever unconsciously gravitate toward someone who seems to have special status.[3] Our culture worships idols. Don't make your friend into one.

3. **Thou shalt not talk about thy friend in her absence as thou wouldst not in her presence.** Protect your friend in the presence of others. Don't say things that reflect negatively on her if you haven't taken them to her first.[4] Her name needs to be safe in your mouth. And guard those prayer requests! Without prior permission, her story is not yours to tell.

4. **Remember thy friend's special days, to keep them happy.** The attribute of friendship I cherish most is thoughtfulness. Not just the obligatory birthday card or call but to know a

friend is "full of thought" for you and you're not just their afterthought. Time is a gift without price.[5]

5. **Honor thy friend's father and mother and spouse and children.** I'll never forget the Saturday when I took our five preteens and an elderly friend to the local mall. My friend Catherine, a highly successful businesswoman who hated shopping, was running a quick errand when she ran into us—me all frazzled and octopus-armed, trying to corral my tribe to go home. Without missing a beat, Cath insisted she needed someone to see a kids' movie and get popcorn, and in an instant, all five kids left with her. I tell you this: No greater love hath a woman than to lay down her free time for a friend.[6]

6. **Thou shalt not kill (quench) thy friend's spirit.** Have you ever unintentionally knocked your friend's ideas or dashed her dreams? Have you lectured when she needed you to listen instead?[7]

7. **Thou shalt not be unfaithful to thy friend, forsaking her friendship for another's.** Loyalty.[8] Along with thoughtfulness, is there any quality more important than this one?

8. **Thou shalt not take from thy friend time that rightfully belongs to another.** Friendship is considerate, not controlling.[9] We shouldn't take time that belongs to a friend's family. My longtime friend Debbie forgave me ages ago, but I still ruefully recall the time I kept her on the phone for *four hours.* And we both had small children! (They all survived, thanks be to God.)

9. **Thou shalt not lead thy friend into gossip.** Our culture no

longer takes gossip seriously, but it's a big deal to God.[10] We might call it sharing or "concern," but if we casually conduct unconstrained conversations about others that we wouldn't have in their presence, it's scuttlebutt. Scuttle it.

10. **Thou shalt not envy thy friend's good fortune but rejoice with her.** Jealousy between friends? It happens, and it's ugly. Even as we share in our friend's pain, we also need to be glad, genuinely glad, when she is honored.[11]

Observing these friendship commandments may be as challenging as keeping the original ten, but we'll be better for it.

And so will our friends.

Points of Connection

1. Look at the first three "commandments." Have you ever elevated a relationship above Christ's lordship? How can we avoid favoring others who can return the favor in some way? What are some practical ways we can protect our friends in the presence of others?

2. Review the next three principles. What are some ways we can demonstrate thoughtfulness in our friendships? How can we "honor" a friend's family? Listening is one of the greatest gifts we can give a friend. Can you recall a time when you were given that gift?

3. As time permits, consider the final four commandments: loyalty, consideration of others' time, constructive conversation, and avoiding envy. Which areas do you potentially need to work on?

Remember Mom's advice? It's still true. The best way to have a friend is to be one.

JUDGING. NOT.

[Jesus said,] "Don't be hypercritical; use your head—and heart!—
to discern what is right, to test what is authentically right."

JOHN 7:24, MSG

FOR A WOMAN not athletically inclined whatsoever, I sure can jump
to conclusions.

Throughout my late twenties and well into my thirties, I taught
communications classes at a small university in New England.
Finances were tight in our ministry household, so whenever I had
the opportunity to pick up extra night classes, I did. While my daytime students were all younger than I was, those continuing their
education in the evenings were significantly older. It was easy to be
intimidated by their age and experience.

A student I'll call Deborah was a challenge from the start.
She sat in the same seat in the back each class session, refusing to
engage in discussion during my lectures, a perpetual scowl on her
face. Hand propped on fist, she stared me down week after week
until I was so unnerved, I began to dread her presence.

She hates me, I thought. *She thinks I'm too young and unqualified*

to be teaching experienced professionals. She'll give me a terrible evalua-
tion, and that will be the end of my tenure in adult education.

After several weeks of our silent confrontations, I asked Deborah to remain after class one evening, and I shared my concerns. Had I said or done anything that offended her?

Deborah was astonished. "Professor Rowe," she blurted out, "I actually look forward to this class. I have an awful work situation and pressures at home. This classroom is a refuge for me. I had no idea I was making you uncomfortable!"

I had made the situation about me, yet it was my student who was struggling. How much I had to learn!

Who else have I been mistaken about lately? The slouchy young man in the hoodie with the tats? The goth teen with shocking-pink hair? That older woman at church whose sour expression hides a kind heart?

Jesus couldn't have been clearer when he rebuked a crowd who accused him of being demon-possessed: "Look beneath the surface so you can judge correctly."[1]

Does this mean we're never supposed to judge others?

Sometimes obeying God necessitates making a judgment, as when Paul warns the church about sexual immorality and the need for careful discernment within the body of believers.[2] Scripture also instructs us to discipline a believer caught in sin with the goal of restoration.[3] Correcting others requires a careful look within in order to render a proper judgment without.

But judging other people's motives or intentions based on our own faulty filters is a wrongheaded way to view the world. We need to be careful not to impound others in the past as if they are the same individuals now that they were then. When it comes to our own previous errors of judgment, most of us make pretty good defense attorneys, but it sure can be tempting to act as both judge and jury when it comes to condemning others for their mistakes.

Only when we finally admit we've been wrong will we get it right. Let's choose to look beneath the surface.

Points of Connection

1. When are you most tempted to render a quick judgment about another person or situation? Did something about the way you were raised predispose you to regard certain ethnic, religious, or political groups as suspect? What safeguards can you put in place going forward to prevent snap judgments?

2. Think of a time in the past when you know you misjudged another person or circumstance. How could you have avoided a rush to judgment? Read 2 Timothy 2:23-26 for some practical instructions on how to treat others.

3. Have you ever seen an insect fossilized in a piece of clear amber? Our judgments of others, however we pretty them up in order to justify our conclusions, can freeze them in a past they no longer inhabit. What steps can we take to give others the grace we long for ourselves?

LifeLine

Resist the temptation to judge by how situations, or people, may first appear. It's when we admit we've been wrong that we finally get it right.

PRICKLY PEOPLE
(AND OTHER PROBLEMS . . .)

*Be agreeable, be sympathetic, be loving, be compassionate, be humble. That goes
for all of you, no exceptions. No retaliation. No sharp-tongued sarcasm. Instead,
bless—that's your job, to bless. You'll be a blessing and also get a blessing.*

I PETER 3:8-9, MSG

IN THE CIRCLE OF LIFE, much that is old becomes new again, sometimes just with a different name. Christians enjoyed fellowship for
generations and practiced it in "fellowship halls" until the name
gave way to "community." The concept is the same, though: the
sense of affinity we develop with others who share common interests, core identities, or mutual goals.

Community is a fabulous thing. Finding commonality with
others alleviates the loneliness we may find ourselves in. Meeting
new people who may potentially become fast friends makes
the neighborhood, gym, or office a more welcoming place.
Community forms the fabric of our lives.

Until it rips.

I hope no one has ever labeled you their "thorn in the flesh."
I've been called worse, but never that. But have I experienced

human thorns? Prickly individuals who seemed bent on consigning me to that particular destination? Yep, and I bet you have too.

I've written elsewhere[1] that the thorn Paul mentioned in his second letter to the Corinthians may have been a physical ailment or chronic illness.[2] Bible commentaries are divided on that. Maybe I've been in pastoral ministry too long, *ahem*, but I've always suspected Paul's thorn was an individual or group who opposed his ministry. For Paul, furtherance of the gospel message was imperative. It makes sense that Satan would deploy a "messenger" to derail the work.

Responding to garden-variety conflict and criticism is one thing, but what do you do when someone positions themselves as your perpetual opponent? Whatever you do and wherever you go, they seem to be there too, watching and waiting for you to stumble. Determined to do whatever they can to make you look bad, to suffer.

By nature, I'm a people person who cares deeply about relationships. Always have. But every once in a while, I feel like *Peanuts* cartoon philosopher Linus van Pelt: "I love mankind . . . It's *people* I can't stand."[3]

On the off chance you happen to have a human thorn impaled in your flesh, how should you respond?

Several places in the New Testament acknowledge that we should try to live at peace *as much as it's up to us*, but resolving difficult situations isn't always possible.[4] Scripture is clear that it's okay for us to request the thorn be removed, whatever that takes. We're encouraged to ask, seek, and knock—a progression of intercession.[5] Paul pleaded with God to take his thorn away, using the Greek verb form *parakaleō*, meaning "to call to one's side for aid."[6] He begged, but for whatever reason God said no.

We're not often given the reason why we're suffering, whether it's at the hand of a human adversary or a physical illness, but in Paul's case, he had a pretty good idea: "to keep me from becoming conceited."[7] God loved Paul too much to allow him to stumble over his own pride.[8]

Along with realizing it's okay to ask God to remove the thorn, we also need to recognize that whether he does so or not, his grace is sufficient for our needs. His unmerited favor is *enough*—not too much, not too little—and, like manna in the wilderness, it is given at the time we need it, not before. Beth Moore has said that whether God chooses to remove a thorn depends on the point: to teach supremacy (he can do it) or sufficiency (he can get us through it).[9] It's often the latter.

Accepting the "point" of a thorn leads to a reorganization of our thinking, doesn't it? My friend Cynthia has often reminded me in times of crisis that we don't need to be strong all the time—because we serve a strong God. In an era when physical prowess or emotional toughness grants bragging rights, divine love flips that temptation on its head. God's power is made perfect in our weakness, not our strength.[10]

Finally, when things get ugly, it's vital we refrain from responding in kind. Scripture is adamant that we not return "evil with evil or insults with insults."[11] During the 2016 presidential campaign, former First Lady Michelle Obama was widely quoted as saying, "When they go low, we go high."[12] We don't refuse to retaliate out of a sense of moral superiority but out of divine strength. When we lob verbal grenades back at the thorns in our lives, we only escalate the situation.

If thorns were introduced into the world because of the sin of Adam, the first man, the curse was removed because of Jesus

Christ, the second Adam.[13] Jesus bore the curse for our sake and wore it as well, a curse symbolized by a crown of thorns.[14] And when those thorns are composed of human flesh, it helps to remember that he died for their sake as well as our own.

Do you feel like thanking God for your thorn today?[15] Nope, me neither. But let's do it anyway—based not our feelings but our faith.

Points of Connection

1. I wish we lived in a world without thorns, human or otherwise. And we will someday. But until then, what can you take away from today's reflection that might help you deal with the thorny situation you're currently in?

2. Jesus, King of the Universe, went to death on a cross—wearing a crown made not of gleaming gold but bloody briars. How does Jesus' experience with thorns speak into your own?

Life Line

Thank God for the thorn in your life, based not on your feelings but your faith.

FRIENDSHIP FAIL

Faithful are the wounds of a friend; but the kisses of an enemy are deceitful.

PROVERBS 27:6, KJV

IT HAPPENED YEARS AGO, but the memory still rankles.

Ana[1] and I were small-group leaders in a community Bible study who had a lot in common. Or so I thought. I welcomed her family when they moved into town and was thrilled when she joined our leadership team. Our families shared meals together, plus a common vision for God's work in our area. It was a promising new friendship.

Until it wasn't.

A divergence of opinion arose among our leaders about the correct interpretation of scriptural passages dealing with women's roles in the church. As the discussion began to generate more heat than light, Ana shared something she'd heard that discredited the study's author, a well-known scholar I had studied under. Heartsick, I did a little research only to discover to my relief the rumor was false.

I was eager to set the record straight, but not in a way that would embarrass Ana in front of the group. I phoned her instead, expressing my appreciation for her leadership, assuming she'd be as happy as I was to know the negative information about the author was false. After a long pause, she hung up the phone, but not before muttering a derogatory term used for, shall we say, female dogs or bad-tempered women. Me? One of those? Stunned, I waited for Ana to apologize the next week, but an apology didn't come. She never spoke to me again.

Maybe this has happened to you too. A minor disagreement with a longtime friend becomes a major blowup. A close buddy you roomed or worked or worshiped with grows distant, and you're left puzzling out where the relationship went south. An F in your BFF changes from "forever" to "former."

When a valued friendship derails, the damage may take months or even years to mend. Sadly, it might be beyond repair. And the pain that follows the loss is immense. Reflecting on the ability people have to work together, journalist Michael Finkel writes, "Human brains are wired to connect—magnetic resonance imaging shows that the same neural circuitry that causes us to feel physical pain is activated when we face social pain, like being shunned from a group or picked last on the playground."[2]

Is there anything we can learn from friendship fail?

First, consider context, yours *and* hers. Did the situation that initiated the fallout really catch you unaware, or were there warning signs you disregarded? Think about what your friend may have been going through at the time. In retrospect, I realized a significant loss Ana had experienced in the previous year may have weakened her tolerance for conflict of any kind, however seemingly insignificant.

Second, what about the not-so-great expectations you had about this friendship? Did you assume her need for a close friend would parallel yours? Though you never consciously kept score, were you irritated that the friendship lacked reciprocity? Unstated expectations are unfair expectations in relationships of all kinds.

In hindsight, I also recognized that while Ana joined our community study as a newcomer, I had been a part of the group for years. Trust and respect were already established among the members, and she may have felt unsure of her place in the mix. Despite my initial attempts to welcome her in, the ugly truth is that we felt threatened by each other.

So her muttered epithet and refusal to speak to me again ended our friendship, right? She was clearly in the wrong.

Except that's not the end of the story. The inconvenient truth is that the biggest failure was my own.

Wanting to validate my wounded feelings, I shared the incident a week later with a trusted friend, Joanna.[3] Jo listened quietly, saying little, but she called me the next day. "Maggie," she said gently, "I know you were hurt, but telling me was not necessary. I did not need to know what Ana said; you must have known it would reflect badly on her."

Well, of course I did—that's why I shared it! After I stopped defending myself, though, and considered what Jo said, I knew she was right. Ana had spoken disparagingly only to me, but I spoke badly of her to another. Her name was not safe in my mouth.

The friendship fail was on me.

The broken friendship with Ana never mended. But I continue to thank God for Joanna's faithful, gutsy friendship. She knew the greatest temptation to sin can come after we've been sinned against, and she cared enough to compassionately confront me.

Faithful are the wounds of a friend.

Points of Connection

1. Friendships bring some of the greatest joy and the deepest pain we experience in interpersonal relationships. Can you remember a time when you were at fault and someone cared enough to risk your friendship by confronting you? How did you respond?

2. Read the following verses and reflect on what they have to teach us about the value of friendship: Proverbs 19:4-6; Ecclesiastes 4:9-12; Titus 2:3-5.

3. Matthew 6:33 reads, "Seek first his kingdom and his righteousness, and all these things will be given to you as well." How might this apply to the friendships we long to have?

LifeLine

The greatest temptation to sin can come after we've been sinned against.

REFLECTION 29

DOES ANYONE WANT TO MENTOR ME?

Take the old prophets as your mentors. They put up with anything, went through everything, and never once quit, all the time honoring God. What a gift life is to those who stay the course! You've heard, of course, of Job's staying power, and you know how God brought it all together for him at the end. That's because God cares, cares right down to the last detail.

JAMES 5:10-11, MSG

LONG BEFORE I KNEW WHAT A MENTOR WAS, I benefited from older women and men who saw qualities in me that I never saw in myself. The fourth-grade teacher who offered to sponsor me in a writing program when I graduated. My first boss out of college, a gentle man soon to retire who hired me to succeed him in his advocacy work for Christian workers overseas. A wonderfully wise pastor's wife who demonstrated by example what a high call and high privilege ministry can be, even when it initially terrified me.

A mentor is someone a few steps ahead on the path who can hold out a hand vocationally or offer a listening ear relationally. In this diverse world of ours, I'm sure there are those who have never wanted or needed that kind of person, but I simply don't know anyone who truly *is* self-made and completely self-sufficient.

If you're seeking someone to come alongside you in a mentoring relationship, the apostle James offers sound advice: Find an old prophet to set the example.[1] But what if you can't locate one (other than in Scripture, of course)? Have you ever considered a mentor might be waiting for someone just like *you*?

In *Lean In*, Sheryl Sandberg references a comment once made by Oprah Winfrey: "I mentor when I see something and say, 'I want to see that grow.'"[2]

For several years, I met regularly with a woman thirty years my junior, whom I knew through church. After a sermon on mentoring, Patricia had approached my husband and me in the foyer. "Being a Christian in my office is really hard," she said in frustration. "Is there someone I can meet with to talk about workplace issues?"

Our women's ministry team had just compiled a list of "Titus 2" mentors—older women willing to come alongside younger. I could have asked a dozen women to work with Patricia. Between full-time work, ministry, and a grad program I was completing at the time, I didn't think I had the margin to do so myself.

But several years later, Patricia and I were still meeting. Why? Because I recognized in this young woman's keen intelligence and transparency remarkable potential for spiritual growth. In turn, Patricia helped me view faith and culture through the eyes of a millennial. "The strongest relationships spring out of a real and often earned connection felt by both sides," writes Sandberg.[3]

At age eighty-two, African American ballet pioneer Raven Wilkinson spoke of the time she first saw ballerina Misty Copeland in a television documentary when Misty was only a young teen. "I got on my knees right there and prayed," commented Raven. "I said, 'Please bless this young girl and let her go on and develop.'" The two dancers did not meet in person until thirteen years later. Though they are separated in age by nearly fifty years, Raven and Misty talked often and met whenever they could.[4] Misty said, "She . . . made me stop looking at myself as just a black ballerina."[5]

Wouldn't it be ideal if each of us could be mentored while simultaneously mentoring a younger woman ourselves? But whether or not someone fills that role for you, you have a lot to offer someone else.

Mentoring is not about being a role model or Bible Answerwoman. It has nothing to do with keeping the perfect home or being übersuccessful at a job. A mentor is one who listens rather than lectures. A mentor resists the temptation, however well intended, to try to fix her mentee's problems. A mentor prays, encourages, and when necessary, gently corrects. A mentor has the humility to admit that she possesses few answers herself, but she's willing to dig deep into life and Scripture to help another woman find them.

Ask the Lord to point the way to a potential mentor and prepare to make your own life lessons available to others. What better legacy can we leave than building into the life of a future leader?

Points of Connection

1. The relationship between Naomi and her daughter-in-law Ruth in the Old Testament, and Mary of Nazareth and her older cousin Elizabeth in the New, are often considered examples of mentoring relationships. From what you know of their stories, how were these women's relationships mutually encouraging and beneficial?

2. Consider several Scripture passages that apply to mentoring: Titus 2, Proverbs 27:17, and Romans 1:12. What do these verses convey about the nature of being a mentor? A mentee?

3. If you long for a mentor in your life, watch for an older woman in your church, workplace, or neighborhood who seems approachable and has life experiences beyond your own. Invite her for coffee with no expectations other than getting together to chat. You might discover she's been praying for someone exactly like you!

Life Line

Spiritual connections that enrich the soul can arise from the most surprising places.

MOVING ON AFTER MOVING IN

All praise to the God and Father of our Master, Jesus the Messiah!
Father of all mercy! God of all healing counsel! He comes alongside
us when we go through hard times, and before you know it, he brings
us alongside someone else who is going through hard times so that
we can be there for that person just as God was there for us.

2 CORINTHIANS 1:3-4, MSG

IN THE YARD OF HER NEW HOME IN COLORADO, my friend Pam has
planted a six-foot-tall post with twenty hand-painted signs pointing
north, south, east, and west. Each whimsical sign bears the name of
a place she has lived, from Chicago to Istanbul, reminding her of all
the locations that brought her and her husband, Pete, to where they
are now.

"Moving all over the world has been quite the adventure," she
comments, "but it's exhausting starting over each time. I'm ready to
put down roots and stay put!"

Whether you're a veteran of dozens of moves (like Pam) or just
a few, you've experienced what it's like to throw your entire life
into boxes and try to make sense of them, and your life, when you
resurface in a new place. Getting to know a different region of the

country or the world can be exciting, but relocation often brings with it a deep sense of loss and disorientation.

If you had a long history and deep friendships in your former location, separation from the known and the familiar can be agonizing, but even an anticipated and entirely welcome move comes as a shock to the system. All the systems. Everything that gave structure and form and purpose to your former life has been dismantled and needs to be rebuilt.

Moving to a different home in the same community is stressful enough. The sorting. The donating and discarding of possessions. The packing.

Relocating to a different state, region, or country kicks the stress level up to a new level. Almost nothing in your life remains the same. New utilities. New insurance coverages of every kind. Different schools, stores, and services. You might need to learn a new language and struggle with asking for directions, not to mention with making friends.

With any relocation, the biggest challenge is to satisfy the most compelling need of all: to belong. Why is our need to know and be known such a powerful one?

At its best, the longing to belong is a positive force for good. We build communities for mutual support. We seek fellowship to know we're not alone. We want to fit in, be useful to others, have a purpose and a place.

At its worst, the drive to belong can become destructive. Tribalism divides neighbor from neighbor because of ethnic identification or misguided loyalty. Political affiliation creates an uncivil war on social media. Gangs become a toxic family, encouraging darker impulses.

Yet the need to belong remains legitimate. Relocation changes the equation of our lives, for a time at least, from one of addition and multiplication to subtraction and perhaps even division, with your loyalties divided between your old friends and the new ones you're getting to know.

If this is where you're at right now, I understand. I'm writing these words just weeks after moving to a brand-new community where I know absolutely no one.

Do you know what was unexpectedly difficult? Taking out my wallet and key ring and cutting up my former library card, store-loyalty tags, and fitness-center ID. I had already surrendered my employee-access card with the chip that beeped me into my office building each day.

Silly to hang on to them, right? Stupidly sentimental, and impractical besides. They had no value except as symbols of former belonging to a people and a place.

Here's what I'm learning to do. I hope these tips will help you, too.

Acknowledge the loss that change brings. "It's called grief. Lament. And it's perfectly normal in these circumstances," my friend Cindy told me following our move. "God knows. Keep weeping and talking to him about change and loss."

Another longtime friend, Melissa, wrote, "Change is hard, scary, and an unknown entity. Time moves on and brings change with it, wiping the slate one more time, often with our tears."

Choose to know, even if not yet to be known. On Saturdays, I march myself to the local farmers' market to chat with the vendors. Jana sells organic poultry. Eddie has the best lettuce and tomatoes. Hank has fresh trout. I drive downtown and duck in and out of the shops, chatting with Ellie at the resale shop or Jackie, the former mayor's wife who's recovering from foot surgery while running the antique store. I've attended a few community festivals and checked

141

out the local library. I'm getting to know people, even if they do not yet know me.

Don't wait to be invited. Issue those invitations yourself, girl! Is your place still a heap? Boxes everywhere? A mess is easier to deal with than loneliness. Let the unpacking go, and invite your new neighbors over to pull up a box and sit down for cookies and conversation. They're curious about you, too, and most likely they'll be happy to offer information about your new area.

Volunteer! Helpers are welcome everywhere. Our new hometown has an excellent community theatre, and I've signed up to get involved. My husband is helping coach the local aquatics club. We're settling into a wonderful new church home and are finding ways to be of service there, too.

And that wallet that relocation emptied in more ways than one? This week I added a new library card, sports-center ID, and a couple of store-loyalty cards. When the grocery-store clerk asked for my card, I was proud to give it to her. Made me feel like a local.

Like maybe I belong.

Points of Connection

1. Think back to the last time you moved, whether it was from your childhood home, into a dorm or an apartment, a job-related transfer to a new community, or maybe relocation accompanying retirement. What helped the most with the initial adjustment?

2. Pick up a copy of a local paper or do some research online to find the event calendar for your community. Take a break from unpacking and attend a concert, play, or workshop at the

library. Chat with those sitting nearby. You might just discover they're new too.

3. Reach out to someone—a neighbor, new coworker, or classmate—and invite them to meet you for coffee. It's hard taking the initiative, but so worth the risk!

Life Line

When you're longing to belong, to find community, ask God to give you the boldness to reach out to others.

RIDING TANDEM

Submit to one another out of reverence for Christ.

EPHESIANS 5:21, NLT

TIRED OF RIDING SOLO? Think the journey would be a breeze on a bicycle-built-for-two?

It's not as easy as you think.

For my guy and me, morning worship is the apex of our Sabbath. A recent Sunday afternoon sloped off like any ordinary day until a scheduled meeting was postponed, and suddenly the time previously spoken for broke open like a geode.

Blessed with a gift of hours, we grabbed a gift certificate to a local cyclery that had been gathering dust in the bureau drawer.

"Are you open today?"

Yes—until four.

"On our way!"

When we arrived, the unusually fine day had claimed most of the rental bikes, and the only one left was a tandem, a bicycle-built-for-two.

But if anything's easier than peddling a two-wheeler, it's doing it with four legs, right? With a tire inflated here and a seat adjusted there, we hopped on and set off.

It's harder than it looks.

Maybe you're already married, and while you'd choose your spouse all over again, you've experienced the work a successful marriage partnership entails. Or maybe the one who promised to love you forever remembered his vows at the altar but forgot them when times got tough.

You might still be single, wondering whether God's the one with the bad memory. Has he forgotten your heart's desire for someone to cherish you above all others? Most of your friends from college have paired off by now. Will there ever be anyone special for you?

I hear you, and you're not alone. I know friends and family members in each of those places and then some. Their stories aren't mine to tell, but after forty-plus years, Mike and I have learned a bit about riding tandem.

It's natural to wobble at first. You're working as a team now. It takes time and practice to learn the rhythms of grace necessary when riding with a partner.

The first big argument Mike and I had, about six months into marriage, was how we'd celebrate Christmas. Would we observe traditions the way his family had (wrong!) or the way mine did (the right way, of course)? We argued the point down to how long the needles on the tree should be. Another blowup had to do with my unstated expectations about our first-anniversary plans.

Before we hopped aboard our tandem bike, the technician advised us to lean into the curves. The pastor who did our premarital counseling said the same thing. Life throws those at you. If you're bending one way and your spouse insists on the other, slow down and get your signals straight. And another tip for the road? Yield to each other when you get to an intersection where the right-of-way is unclear. Two vehicles or people can't occupy the same space at the same time, or there will be major conflict.

Prepare properly before you set out. We're grown-ups, right? People have been riding bikes since forever, so who needs advice? We did. "You won't get far with a chain like that," the technician observed. We listened, made some adjustments, and were better for it. How many relationships might have been saved if the couple spent more time preparing for the marriage than they did for the details of the wedding day?

Riding tandem gets easier with practice. (Gosh, tell us something new, please.) But it's true. Farther down the bike path, we were starting to peddle in sync. And after decades of marriage, we've learned to put each other's needs above our own. In some crazy, strange way, we both win.

So yeah, you go faster alone, but you travel farther together.

And those riding partners who bail out or push you off? It happens, and it stinks. But the journey's not over.

"So how did it go?" the technician asked when we returned, laughing and a bit out of breath. "Worth the ride or wish you'd gone solo?"

We've been riding tandem for over forty years, Mr. Bike Man. And yes, it's been worth the ride.

Every mile and every minute.

Points of Connection

1. Today's verse is taken from a longer passage on marriage in Paul's letter to the Ephesians. Read Ephesians 5:21-28 in several modern translations. The word *submit*, with its English

connotation of dominance, is often a source of contention. In the original Greek, the word is *hupotassō*, and among other things, it conveys the concept of "coordinating with or aligning under." Spouses are to work together toward a common objective, "submitting to others according to the authority and order established by God."[1] What common objective do you see as central to the direction of your marriage? If you were to write a mission statement for your marriage, what would it be?

2. Psalm 45:10-15 (MSG) contains a beautiful description of a royal wedding (gold-lined bridal gown, anyone?). While none of us will have a human marriage quite like this, Scripture often compares the relationship between husband and wife to the one between Christ—the Bridegroom—and his people, the church. How might your marriage better reflect this description of the eternal marriage?

3. Like anything of great value, the marriage relationship will come under spiritual attack. How does Ephesians 6:10-18 instruct believers to prepare for and remain strong during times of conflict and testing?

LifeLine

Marriage was God's idea from the very beginning. Riding tandem takes practice, but it's worth every mile and every minute.

PUTTING THE SALSA BACK IN YOUR MARRIAGE

Wives, understand and support your husbands in
ways that show your support for Christ.

EPHESIANS 5:22, MSG

IN A SEASON-TWO EPISODE OF THE NETFLIX SERIES *The Crown,*
Queen Elizabeth suggests to her husband that they plan a tenth-
anniversary celebration. Philip is noncommittal, but Elizabeth is
clearly concerned that the pressures of the monarchy are driving
them apart. The camera follows the pair as they silently ascend the
palace staircase to their separate rooms, parting at the top with a
subdued good night.

You don't have to be queen to know that marriage has its challenges. My husband and I have done premarital counseling with
dozens of young adults who planned their ceremonies fully expect-
ing the happily-ever-after. And why shouldn't they? Who would go
through with a wedding to someone they don't love passionately?
Someone with whom they don't expect to spend the rest of their
life till death do them part?

But between saying yes to the dress (and the guy) and the fairy-tale ending, life happens. People are unpredictable, emotions are fickle, and feelings fade. How do you put the spice, the *salsa* back in your marriage?

A group of young moms put this question to me not long ago. Their kids were playing together nearby while the moms enjoyed a brief respite from wiping noses and changing diapers. They love their families, but the needs of the kids take every ounce of energy they have. "Honestly, at night all I want is my pillow and a magazine," one commented. "I've got nothing left for him."

Whether you've been married two years, ten, or forty plus (like us), you already know a healthy marriage needs continual care. Here are a few ideas my mom-friends and I generated on keeping marriage interesting, protected, and most of all, thriving.

Create safeguards. Meh, sounds so boring. But what you love, you defend. Instead of prioritizing all the stuff you already have scheduled, try scheduling your priorities instead. Put regular date nights on your calendar. If babysitters aren't in the budget, arrange to occasionally swap childcare with a friend. Or consider asking an empty nester, one without nearby grandkids, to help.

Safeguards include protecting your own heart too. I'm not going to advise you never to be alone with a member of the opposite sex, but let the Holy Spirit guide your conscience. Do you catch yourself being preoccupied by your appearance when you're with a certain OSF (opposite-sex friend)? Do you find yourself thinking about positive attributes he has that you wish your spouse displayed? How about planning and possessiveness? Are you creating opportunities to see your OSF or saving his notes, cards, or emails? Most important, are you allowing your OSF to meet emotional needs your spouse should be meeting?

Adjust expectations. Unstated expectations are unfair expectations. Unexpressed expectations are unrealistic expectations. The problem child here is expectations: assuming, supposing, or presuming your spouse knows what you're thinking, needing, and wanting. And if he doesn't, he darn well should!

When Mike and I were first married, I didn't doubt he loved me (I never have), but I assumed since he did, he should know exactly how I wanted to (a) celebrate our anniversary, (b) share the workload at home, and (c) make financial decisions. Now, Mike is many things, including my best friend, but a mind reader he's not. We've learned how to love each other more deeply by listening without judgment and plainly expressing our feelings and preferences.

Laugh often. Discover what brings delight to your spouse and invest time in it. Funny animal videos on YouTube? A sports team that performs really, really badly? (Not his hometown team!) Watching children play, maybe even your own? Science has repeatedly proven the physical and emotional benefits of laughter. It strengthens the immune system, releases endorphins that boost mood, reduces stress, and increases energy level.

Prioritize sexual intimacy. Generalizations are risky, but this one's pretty safe. Men are interested in sex, and your guy is turned on by visual stimulation. I know, right? Once the honeymoon's over, who wants to wear the slinky, shivery stuff when warm flannel pj's will do? Men show love physically, though, and he doesn't just want you. He needs you to want him too.[1] Marriage was God's idea in the first place. He created men and women to meet each other's physical as well as emotional needs within the context of a covenantal marriage relationship.

Seek out adventure. Monotony is not a marriage killer, but it can cause couples to doze through the best years. Your marital journey's gotta include adventure: times when you set aside practicality and dream. Together.[2] Then brainstorm how to make those dreams happen without shooting down the crazy ideas your spouse tosses up.

Like I almost did. Mike's dream was to travel for a year after we finished seminary and before we started a family. He's always been the visionary, the dreamer who's pushed the gas pedal while I put on the brakes. I suggested a month. We compromised at four, the limit we could afford to be unemployed. Our modest budget included no hotels or restaurant food. Instead, we pitched our pup tent in national parks all over the country and ate tuna fish out of cans while sitting on the rim of the Grand Canyon. We covered sixteen thousand miles and thirty-four states in our little Honda with no air-conditioning. We have wonderful memories of that trip to this day.

Does your marriage need an extra ingredient or two? I recommend salsa.

Points of Connection

1. God has designed marriage as the union between one man and one woman (Genesis 1:26-27). What a designer creates, he is invested in. How does knowing that God wants your marriage to not only survive but thrive encourage you to press through the tough times?

2. Are there expectations you've had of your spouse that you have never articulated? What are some ways you can make a fresh start communicating more effectively about what you need and want from your marriage and what he needs and wants as well?

3. Read Proverbs 31:12 and 1 Corinthians 13:4-5. These passages on marriage are familiar. How might you read them in light of putting the salsa back in your marriage?

LifeLine

If your marriage is becoming predictable and stale,
try adding a little salsa.

PARTY OF ONE? THIS WAY, PLEASE!

Don't look out only for your own interests,
but take an interest in others, too.

PHILIPPIANS 2:4, NLT

"You can't have a ministry here for women only!" the older woman scolded. "This is a family church, and we don't want any activities that separate couples."

I was shocked at this unexpected reaction from a key lay leader in the nearly two-hundred-year-old church we had been newly called to pastor. When I had asked God how he would have me serve there, I clearly heard his direction: *There is nothing here for my daughters. Start something. Begin with teaching them to love my Word. I will be with you.*

No one could object to a ministry designed to serve over half the adult population of a church, right?

Wrong. I was stunned to face immediate opposition from the most powerful female in the church, one whose strident voice intimidated others into silence. Pointing out that many of our women were unmarried or newly single following divorce or widow-hood made no difference. They were not part of a "nuclear family" and therefore were welcome to serve but were not to be singled out. No gender-based ministry allowed. My orders were to focus on the needs of families alone.

Phooey. (That's about the closest a preacher's wife can get to a curse.) With the strong support of my pastor-husband and a stel-lar group of diverse women who eagerly offered to help, we deter-mined that our church family would minister to the needs of every adult, without regard to marital status. Singles would not only be welcome to serve but welcome, *period*. In the years to come, God began a new work in our church that impacted not only our com-munity but scores of women across the region.

Contrast this with a later church we were privileged to pastor. When the time came to elect a church-council representative of the entire church body, both male and female leaders were appointed. Younger and older. Married and single. And the individual chosen as chairperson just happened to be single. Larissa wasn't selected because the apostle Paul said the single state is to be preferred[1] or because she had any more time available than those with kids at home. Larissa led because she was gifted with the character and credentials to do so. The entire church benefited from her capable, compassionate leadership.

Despite Paul's wish that everyone would remain unmarried, the church has had a complicated relationship with its singletons. Mandy Hale, creator of The Single Woman, a social-media move-ment, comments: "Why is [the church and singleness] rather like oil and water? Like Chick-fil-A and Sundays? Like me and kale? Why do the two just seem to not fit together no matter how des-perately we might want them to?"[2]

Author Joy Beth Smith writes that one of the first things that we need to change in the church is our language: the way we speak to and about singles. She wishes that, instead of asking about her love life (or lack of it), the married women in her church would engage her in conversation about her work or her interest in foster care: "Those are the kinds of questions that reinforce my worth and contributions right now, not the role of wife and mother I could potentially adopt."[3]

My friend Sharon is single again after her husband left their twenty-five-year marriage for another woman. Loneliness is her most frequent companion, so Sharon appreciates it when others make an effort to include her. What makes her wince, though, is when married friends insist they know how she feels because their husbands occasionally travel (which also happens to be the only time they reach out). None of us should blithely say we know how a single woman feels unless we've been there too.

Ministries designed specifically for singles get a mixed review. When our oldest son, Adam, was single and on staff at a large church in California, he enjoyed their "1835" gatherings, events organized around varied activities of interest to high-school grads as well as singles in their thirties. For others, singles ministries are highly uncomfortable, as if they're a "meat market" designed to troll for dates. My friend Alyssa,[4] an attractive twenty-seven-year-old, attended singles events at her new church in Colorado, hoping to make friends. She was forced to find a new church when several of the other single women looked at her darkly and told her to "stay away" from the few available men.

Women who have experienced the trauma of divorce or widowhood sometimes feel marginalized in faith communities as well, however inclusive the leadership is. One friend told me of small groups that rejected a prospective new member simply because she was not part of a couple. Others look on divorced women with mistrust or even suspicion, as if their presence might threaten the marriages in the group. Still other churches, though, intentionally make space for those who are newly single. My mom, who is ninety-four, was drawn to her new church in the Smokies in part because they welcomed her to a widows' group that meets regularly.

God is the Author of marriage. Healthy marriages reflect the marvelous, mystical union between God and his church. But those who are not yet or are no longer in a marital relationship must be equally valued as cherished members of the body of Christ—for "Christ is the only spouse that can truly fulfill us and God's family the only family that will truly embrace and satisfy us."[5]

Whether you are single, married, or single again, a party of one or four or seven, know that you have a place at God's table. We need one another.

Welcome!

Points of Connection

1. If you're single or single again, what have you experienced as part of a faith community? How can ministry leaders help singles truly feel at home within the walls of the church?

2. If you're married, brainstorm ways you can make sure your single friends are remembered and valued. Write a note or call them on days that might be especially tender: the anniversary of a divorce or a spouse's death. Send valentines in February. Leave candy on the desks of single coworkers. Invite them to join you for a meal at home with your family.

3. Above all else, practice the ministry of presence. Be available to listen without offering advice when your friend needs to verbally process the loss of a marriage or her longing for a spouse.

LifeLine

Single out your single friends by welcoming them into every corner of life, especially the church.

CRADLES AND THE CROSS

Again Jesus said, "Simon son of John, do you love me?"
He answered, "Yes, Lord, you know that I love you."
Jesus said, "Take care of my sheep."

JOHN 21:16

LAST WEEK, I TOOK CARE OF MY GRANDSON while my son and
daughter-in-law were at work. We live hundreds of miles apart,
and I welcome opportunities to help them when we visit. My
husband and I raised three children from scratch, plus a couple of
bonus kids who arrived as tweens—half-baked, as we like to tease
them.

With all that experience, I thought I was plenty prepared for
the grandparent gig—long days in which you get nothing done
but ensuring the baby's survival: making meals, changing diapers,
picking up toys, cleaning up messes, giving baths, praying, singing,
reading stories even as you struggle to keep your eyes open.

We forget so quickly what it's like to be a caregiver on call 24-7.
Expectant parents usually receive the cliché advice from the veter-
ans: *Hang in there—the days are long, but the years are short. The kids*
will be grown and gone before you know it. They grow up so fast.

That's absolutely true, but when you're stumbling through those 2:00 a.m. feedings, it sure doesn't feel like it.

You might be in the throes of parenting right now, or it could be you've reversed roles and the older adults you depended on are now depending on you. Maybe you're in the sandwich generation, caring for children and aging parents at the very same time. And every bone in your body is exhausted.

Toning spiritual muscles is vital for our well-being, just as regular physical exercise is, but when loved ones' needs dominate the landscape of your days, soul care can be nearly impossible. How do you nurture your spiritual life when caring for others who rely on you takes every ounce of strength you've got?

In her aptly named book *Long Days of Small Things*, Catherine McNiel describes the dilemma:

> My responsibilities [as a mom] rarely allow me to shower, much less sharpen spiritual practices. Silence and solitude? Never, ever, day or night. Prayer? Harder than you'd think after years of sleep deprivation. Fasting? Not while pregnant or breastfeeding.[1]

If your days are spent at home caring for young children, aging parents, or a spouse with declining health, you're well aware of the limitations full-time caregiving poses. Unless you have family nearby to help or can afford respite care, it might be impossible for you to join a Bible study or participate in a faith community on a regular basis. Social-media feeds where friends post engaging photos of their activities only exacerbate the isolation you're experiencing.

But what if the activities that already define your days are refining your soul in the process?

McNiel writes,

Though we mamas may appear half crazed, sleep-deprived, harried, and unkempt, our souls are being taught and sharpened and purified. . . . We're not able to sit and ponder this, or even be aware of it most of the time. But soul refining is the work of struggle, sacrifice, discomfort, and perseverance. My [children] take me to the end of myself on a daily basis, and I'm certain my soul will emerge stronger for it.[2]

Irish missionary, writer, and social reformer Amy Carmichael went to India initially to do the work of an evangelist, but eventually, she found herself caring for hundreds of children as well.

According to biographer Elisabeth Elliot, Amy had gone to India to bring the message of the Cross, not to rock cradles, but "It is not the business of the servant to decide what work is great, which is small, which important or unimportant."[3] The saving of children became a fire in Amy's bones.

Through the sacrificial work you do in caring for others, your soul is being strengthened every day. As you feed his lambs, the Great Shepherd is nurturing you, too.

Points of Connection

1. Think through your responsibilities on a typical day (if there is such a thing). How does caring for your loved ones cultivate your prayer life and bring you closer to God?

2. Throughout the ages, the people of God have practiced spiritual disciplines, including intercessory and contemplative

prayer, solitude, Bible study, meditation, and acts of service. Which of these feel impossible in your present life stage? Identify several ways in which you might already be practicing these disciplines outside a structured framework.

3. Martin Luther King Jr. once said, "Everybody can be great because anybody can serve. You don't have to have a college degree to serve. You don't have to make your subject and verb agree to serve. You only need a heart full of grace. A soul generated by love."[4] How does this statement reflect Jesus' teaching on caring for others? See Matthew 25:40-45 and Luke 10:25-37.

Life Line

When caregiving contains no quiet or time, rest in the presence of the one who is caring for you.

LORD, LET MY KIDS GET CAUGHT

God is educating you; that's why you must never drop out. He's treating you as dear children. This trouble you're in isn't punishment; it's training, the normal experience of children. Only irresponsible parents leave children to fend for themselves. Would you prefer an irresponsible God? We respect our own parents for training and not spoiling us, so why not embrace God's training so we can truly live?

HEBREWS 12:7-9, MSG

A MOUSE TAUGHT ME to make my bed.

My mother tried her hardest to instill that discipline in me, but the wheezing coal furnace of our century-old farmhouse delivered scant heat to our second-floor bedrooms. At night, my sibs and I argued over whose turn it was to run upstairs during the brutally cold midwestern winters to switch on the electric blankets. Why shiver in the mornings while making a bed that no one would see until I crawled into it again that night?

Until that time I dove under the covers one January night to find a mouse had sought the warmth of my bed before me. My shrieking exit was all it took to convince me of the merits of pulling the covers up tight every morning after that.

It's a comical memory, yet it helped to fuel my parenting

philosophy when I became a mom years later. All kids disobey at times when they think no one will notice. It was my fervent prayer, especially during their teenage years, that they'd get caught before bringing permanent harm to themselves or others in matters much more consequential than the making of a bed.

"Lord," I would pray, "if the kids are rebelling against what we've asked them to do, please send a mouse!"

Better that than the police, but no such luck. The three kids we raised from scratch as well as our bonus kids have made it to adulthood, thankfully. Most got there fairly calmly, but one or two skidded in sideways while we were holding our breath and hollering out prayers. I've been astonished to hear the stories they gleefully swap now at family gatherings about the escapades they pulled off. Some were as innocuous as shooting illegal firecrackers off the back deck, while others had more serious consequences.

But throughout those turbulent teen years, my prayers remained the same. *Let them get caught, Lord, in the small things before they are emboldened to take greater risks. Their dad and I can't be with them every minute, but you are, Lord. You are never more surely with them than when we are not. Send a mouse, a principal, a cop—whatever it takes!*

Scripture tells us, "No discipline is enjoyable while it is happening—it's painful! But afterward there will be a peaceful harvest of right living for those who are trained in this way."[1]

I'm thankful Peter, the great apostle and rock of the church, got caught. Despite Jesus' prediction that Peter would fail him, not once but three times, Peter was confident in his own inner strength. Others might fall away, but Peter? Never.[2]

But what Jesus foresaw took place only hours later. When Peter was recognized as one of Jesus' companions, he tried to divert the conversation. "I don't know what you're talking about," he insisted as he moved away from his inquisitor. (Sound familiar, moms?) When a second woman identified him, Peter denied the truth of her witness, compounding the lie with an oath. "I don't know the man!" Unconvinced, those present called him out with a simple fact: "Your accent gives you away."[3]

Faced with irrefutable proof, Peter escalated his lies a third time, using the strongest language of all—insisting as if he were in a court of law that he did not know Jesus. An innocent person doesn't need to invoke curses as he protests his lack of culpability.

Yet whatever those present thought of Peter's unconvincing disclaimers, he was caught by his own conscience. The cry of a rooster heralding the approach of dawn pierced through the darkness of his denials. Conviction came, swift and shuddering. He had done exactly what he had sworn he'd never do.

This could be the bleak end to Peter's story, or to yours and mine. But look at the hope contained in the next six words: "He went outside and wept bitterly."[4]

God can use our bitter tears of regret and revulsion at our past actions to cleanse us.[5] When we're caught in a web of our own making, or our children are, the regret that leads to repentance is what ultimately leads to spiritual deliverance.[6]

This wasn't the end to Peter's story. God had an extraordinary future in store for this flawed, humbled, gifted man.

As he does for you. And for me. And for our children.

Points of Connection

1. Think back over times in your life when you flouted authority or experienced moral failure. What ultimately led to true repentance and a change of direction?

2. The story of the apostle Peter is ultimately a story of restoration and second chances. What other men and women in Scripture failed God and yet went on to accomplish extraordinary things through their changed lives?

3. Read the following passages: Psalm 37:23-24; Lamentations 3:22-23; 1 Corinthians 10:12-13. What's the common denominator here when it comes to recovering from failure?

Life Line

When your children rebel, pray they'll be caught, and that discipline will lead to their spiritual freedom.

MORE WAYS THAN ONE
TO BE A MOM

Your job is to speak out on the things that make for solid doctrine. . . .
Guide older women into lives of reverence so they end up as neither
gossips nor drunks, but models of goodness. By looking at them, the
younger women will know how to love their husbands and children,
be virtuous and pure, keep a good house, be good wives. We don't want
anyone looking down on God's Message because of their behavior.

TITUS 2:1-6, MSG

HAVE YOU NOTICED THAT NEWS OUTLETS reporting stories of those
tragically killed or missing almost always include parental status,
if the victim had minor children? It's not that being a mother or
father automatically confers greater worth in our culture. But the
impact on society is significant when children lose a parent or
guardian. Those in authority need to make immediate decisions
concerning the physical and emotional well-being of minors.

Scripture tells us our spiritual health is equally important. Those
who are more mature in the faith are explicitly instructed to guide
younger believers. For women, a spiritual mother can be anyone who
is part of the labor process when new life in Christ begins or anyone
who acts as a model or mentor for someone younger in the Lord.

There are many kinds of mothers. The Bible draws no biological boundaries when it comes to sharing their stories. They include traditional moms like Sarah, mother of Isaac; Hannah, Samuel's mother; and Eve, mother of us all. Volumes have been written about Mary of Nazareth, the most famous mother in history.

Spiritual moms described in Scripture include Naomi, mother-in-law to Ruth, whose close relationship prompted the younger woman to declare perpetual fealty.[1] The most well-known mentoring relationship of all is the one described in the gospel of Luke, when Mary visited her pregnant cousin Elizabeth. Nothing is known of Mary's relationship with her parents, but God provided an older female relative who welcomed her warmly and affirmed the angel's astounding message.[2]

Familial ties aside, the Bible also honors women who exemplified strong leadership in a patriarchal culture. Deborah served the children of Israel through her extraordinary gifting as prophet, ruler, warrior, arbiter, and judge.[3] Miriam, along with her younger brothers, Moses and Aaron, was one of the three great leaders of Israel during the period of the Exodus.[4]

What's striking about these stories is the clarity Scripture brings to the subject of true spiritual motherhood. There is no record of Deborah bearing biological children, yet she is called "a mother in Israel."[5] Like Deborah, Miriam fulfilled a prophetic role while also leading the Israelites in worship.

What's most encouraging is that these women were gifted and influential, but certainly not perfect. God himself confronted and disciplined Miriam when she spoke against Moses, yet the record reveals she was restored after a time apart and honored until her death.[6] If we think we need to wait until we're fully mature to fulfill the role of a spiritual mom, we have Miriam's example. She was ninety-plus years old, and God was still working on her!

Being a spiritual mom goes beyond evangelism, helping to birth new life in Christ, just as being a traditional mom goes beyond raising children from birth, fostering, or adoption. We have a responsibility to those who are younger in the faith to nurture and care for them. The ultimate goal? Raising them to resemble our Father.

Beth Moore has said, "Once we fall in love with Christ, we are so taken with His beauty, we want children who look just like Him. That's spiritual motherhood in a nutshell: raising sons and daughters that look just like their Father."[7]

It's not an easy task. It's impossible, actually, without empowerment from the Holy Spirit. An enormous responsibility? Yes, but thankfully, it's our response to *his* ability.

And here's the promise, friends. Even as we tend to our spiritual young, whether in our home, workplace, or classroom, our Great Shepherd is tending us.[8] We have the unfailing love of our Father to see us through.

There are many kinds of moms, and more ways than one to become one. Look around—someone might be praying for a "mom" just like you.

Points of Connection

1. Is there a woman in your life who has served as a spiritual mom to you? What did you value most about her presence in your life? List a few things you've learned from her that you'd like to pass along to others.

2. Read the story of Deborah in Judges 4–5. In what ways can the example of her gifting as prophet, ruler, warrior, and arbiter apply to spiritual motherhood in our present day?

3. Actress Della Reese said in an interview, "My mother was a personal friend of God's. They had ongoing conversations."[9] One of the most powerful ways you can serve your spiritual progeny is by praying for them. How can Jesus' prayer in John 17 serve as a model to pray as he did for protection, unity, joy, and holiness for those you care for?

Life Line

Becoming a spiritual mom is not a matter of biology but theology.
When we love God, we'll love his children, too.

ON PARENTING: HOLDING THEM CLOSE AND LETTING THEM GO

Watch what God does, and then you do it, like children who learn proper behavior from their parents. Mostly what God does is love you. Keep company with him and learn a life of love. Observe how Christ loved us. His love was not cautious but extravagant. He didn't love in order to get something from us but to give everything of himself to us. Love like that.

EPHESIANS 5:1-2, MSG

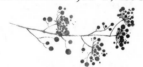

YOU NEVER GET USED TO IT. Not really.

These are the words I need to say to the young parents seated in a circle around us. It's August, and my husband and I are teaching a four-week Sunday-morning class on raising children. We've had our turn, trusted to grow three seedlings from scratch, plus a couple more who arrived half-grown. All grown now and all gone.

Now it's their turn, these fervent younger moms and dads. They ask deeply thoughtful questions about strong-spirited children and softhearted parents. About how to construct family time from sturdy stuff when jobs and schools and kids' soccer practices saw away at the seams. About technology and the teen years and how to say you're sorry.

All good, that. All necessary, mostly. Because they already know by heart what matters: The way that sprout in your arms can tender the toughest of hearts. The mathematical wonder of loving the second or third or sixth child as much as the first. The mystical multiplication of time to care for each new life that slips into yours when those already there take up every moment you have.

So we talk about all of it, and then some. But we don't tell these bright young parents what's barreling toward them on the other side of the highway. It will get here soon enough.

But there were clues, weren't there? We ought to have been suspicious.

It was that wave as your boy disappeared into the yellow maw of a bus on his first day of school. It was the fist raised in triumph as your girl clutched that paper scroll at graduation. It was the kiss blown over a shoulder as you sat in a front pew, all glammed up with your eyes leaking.

A child's coming day is marked with celebration, at least for the fortunate ones who know they're loved. But the going days? How do you let a child go when he takes your heart with him?

The woman Jesus called Mother knew all about that.

Several years ago, I sat on a hill overlooking Nazareth, thinking about Mary. It seemed the right place for pondering. How hard it must have been for her! When the overshadowing came, she became pregnant. But it wasn't until Mary relinquished the plans she had for her child in favor of his Father's that she felt the full weight of what it meant to be his mother.

I can picture her there, standing on top of that same hill. Stepping to the side of Jesus' life when her son began his public ministry. Standing on the fringe of the crowds, raising an unsteady hand in farewell.

It's what we do, isn't it? We hold our offspring close, and then we let them go.

They grow up. The baby can't stay in the manger forever. The Savior entered the world as an infant and left as a man—fully flesh and fully God. He assured those he left behind that separation was only temporary. The world is pregnant with the promise of his coming again.

Those kids who are all grown and all gone? The hands raised in fare-thee-well? Here's what we have to tell younger parents: They'll come back to you again. Yes, they will. With arms full of love and learning and maybe bringing someone new who will root right into your heart.

The world is full of comings and goings. But you make the most of all that comes, and the least of all that goes.

So we hold them close, and then we let them go.

Points of Connection

1. Raising children only to release them into the world when they reach young adulthood is a building project without a blueprint. If you are currently in the parenting years, you already realize that while the days are long, the years are short. What are concrete steps you can take now to maximize the time you have with your children, despite the pressures of making a living?

2. There are many instances in the Gospel accounts where Jesus' mother, Mary, was present during his years of public ministry. Some were celebratory, as when she urged him to help the host of a wedding feast (John 2:1-11). Other occasions, such as his teaching in a private home when his family members

were outside, were confusing (Matthew 12:46-50). And one—Mary's presence at Jesus' crucifixion—was agonizing (John 19:23-30). What might the life of the most famous mother in history teach us about loving children and releasing them to their life callings?

We lead our children, we love them, and we let them go.
No one ever said it would be easy.

GRANDPARENTING IS FOR EVERYONE

The glory of the young is their strength;
the gray hair of experience is the splendor of the old.

PROVERBS 20:29, NLT

BY THE TIME THESE WORDS APPEAR IN PRINT, our fifth grandchild will have joined our family. *Five*, when there was a time not long ago when I worried that we'd never have even one. I am giddy with gratitude.

Much of my longing for grandkids comes from a desire to be what I never had: a caring elder in the life of a child. My father's parents died before I was born, and my mother's lived hundreds of miles away, with health issues that precluded frequent visits.

If you are fortunate enough to still have a grandparent in your life, I hope you've experienced their unconditional, protective love. And if you've already entered this joyful stage of life, you know what can happen.

The first grandchild is born—or the second or fourth or twenty-third—and all Nana/Mimi/Granny wants to do is to gaze enraptured at that baby's face. The world stops at this little one's door. Nothing matters as much as marveling at the miracle of that tiny human.

The media often portrays grandparents as stereotypes: the quintessential older couple rocking in their living room, glasses perched on noses, his head balding, hers crowned with gray. But the reality is that grandparenting today looks vastly different than it used to.

Here are a few things today's grandparents have discovered:

- Running shoes are great for rocking cradles, and jogging strollers make it possible for Grandma to take baby out while training for her own 5K.
- Sending pictures to the family is no longer a matter of having film developed and photos printed and mailed. These days, Grandma has baby in one arm while snapping, texting, and tagging photos on social media with the other.
- Need time off work to help the young parents? No problem: It goes with you. Grandma logs on to her laptop and joins conference calls at the office while baby naps.
- Reading stories to your grandchildren is one of the best ways to introduce them to a lifelong love of books. Nothing beats having that child in your lap, but long-distance grandparents can close the distance through weekly story times via video chats.

Everything has changed about grandparenting. And absolutely nothing has.

The wonder of rediscovering an experience lost in the past; the miracle of life freshly born.

The feeling of a tiny fist clutched around your little finger.

The absolute certainty, swift and fierce, that you would die for this child.

Grandparenting is so critically important it shouldn't be reserved only for those with children who have children.

Along with several other women, my friend Bonnie volunteers at the child enrichment center operating daily on the campus of our church. Bonnie doesn't function as a teacher or even an aide; she's present as a nana. With her own family hundreds of miles away, Bonnie chooses to care for little ones in our local area who need the loving presence of an elder to play a game, cuddle in a chair, or read a story.

Maybe you know of a young couple living far from their families or a single parent who needs support. Come alongside them and offer to babysit, demonstrate a skill, or share a story. Teach a Sunday-school class or assist with a Scout troop. Sign up for nursery rotation at your place of worship so parents have a safe place to leave their kids while they're spiritually refreshed.

Most of all, take what you've learned and press it into the life of a child before you take your knowledge and experience out of time and into eternity.

Grandparenting *is* for everyone.

Points of Connection

1. In our mobile society, many parents are raising children far from their extended families. If you're a grandparent, your own grands might be a community or even a continent away. What are some practical ways you can come alongside parents to provide emotional, physical, and spiritual support?

2. Perhaps you've had a grandparent who has not been present in your life due to time, distance, or lack of interest. You've felt that loss. You may not have children yourself now or any time soon in the future. Are there ways you can build into the lives of the young in your neighborhood or faith community in order to provide for others what you've never had yourself? What can we learn from our own longings?

3. If you are fortunate enough to be a grandparent, don't try to take the place of the parents unless circumstances demand it or they ask you to. Be sensitive about offering advice only when asked. Intervene only when the child's safety or well-being is at stake.

Life Line

Even if you haven't raised kids who have kids, you can still fill the role of a loving elder in the life of a child.

WHAT THE AMISH CAN TEACH US ABOUT HOSPITALITY

*Stay on good terms with each other, held together by love. Be
ready with a meal or a bed when it's needed. Why, some have
extended hospitality to angels without ever knowing it!*

HEBREWS 13:1-2, MSG

"CARE FOR SOME STEW?"

My husband and I were admiring a tidy vegetable garden when
a friendly voice behind us called out the invitation. Turning, we
discovered the speaker: a young Amish man standing in front of an
outdoor fireplace, a long wooden spoon in his hand.

"Sure!" We accepted hearty servings of one of the most aromatic
concoctions I've ever tasted: thick chunks of sausage simmered
with carrots, potatoes, onions, and herbs. The ingredients may have
been garden-variety, but Daryl Yoder's hearty welcome was even
warmer than the stew. [1] We chatted for a few minutes, washed our
food down with cups of cold well water, and were on our way.

We were in northern Indiana for a wedding, and we discovered
we'd arrived on the perfect June day to participate in the third

annual Rentown Garden Walk and Bake Sale—an event held each year to benefit the local one-room schoolhouse. After dropping our donation into a fabric-covered coffee can, we sipped mint-flavored cups of sweet tea and perused the baked goods, farm-fresh eggs, and homemade egg noodles. A smiling schoolgirl, hair tucked beneath a white bonnet, bagged our purchases and gave us a hand-drawn map to the nine homes on the walk.

An avid gardener, my husband was fascinated by the immaculate garden plots tucked far away on country roads. He loved conversing with the Amish families who welcomed us to their homesteads. He questioned them eagerly about soil content and the names of plants unfamiliar to us, while the Amish gardeners responded to his enthusiasm with offerings of their own. Floyd Burkholder sent us on our way with a bag of spearmint leaves for our tea. Mary Hochstetler dug up a perennial we admired and pressed it into our hands. Clara Yoder told us where to order wisteria hardy enough to survive northern winters.

Yet we came away from our garden walk with more than bags stuffed with plant cuttings and bellies full of stew. As we drove to the wedding later that afternoon, Mike and I realized we had experienced biblical hospitality—the art of extending kindness to strangers—at its finest. Here's what we learned about hospitality that day:

- **Hospitality must be a way of life, not an occasional occurrence.** The warm Amish welcome we received flowed naturally out of their culture. It's an "unforced rhythm of grace." Amish children are not shooed away but instead welcomed as guests with their parents, extending cups of cold water and chatting easily without reticence.

- **Hospitality begins with genuine interest in others.** Our hosts quickly turned each conversation to us, wanting to know where we were from and what brought us to the back roads of Rentown. While we quickly found commonality in our mutual love for the land, they were also interested in Mike's calling as a pastor and my childhood as a farmer's daughter. If we felt a bit shy about driving onto their land, they quickly put us at ease. We parted as new friends with promises to return.

- **Hospitality is best when it doesn't seek to impress.** These Amish families were genuine. Saturday is wash day, and their backyard clotheslines were full of barn-door pants, colorful cotton dresses, and children's underwear. No need to hide their laundry from visitors. When I stepped from our Toyota directly into a fresh pile of horse manure, Floyd Burkholder laughed and apologized for failing to clean up his "fuel." He didn't make me uncomfortable by displaying embarrassment.

Hospitality among the Amish is plain, not fancy. It's outwardly focused. And best of all, it's an expression of their faith.

You don't need a bonnet and a buggy to extend a genuine welcome. Pick up a pizza or fire up the grill and invite someone new to join you for a simple meal. The house—and the heart—that's warmed might just be yours.

Points of Connection

1. Do you hesitate to invite people into your home? Is your reluctance due to a lack of time or finances? Do you feel you have to keep your home "company ready"? In what ways might you extend casual hospitality as a natural part of your week?

2. If you didn't grow up in a home with parents who enjoyed hosting guests, can you think of someone you know who seems to have a gift for making others feel at ease in her home? What can you learn from her?

3. Hospitality extends beyond offering others a room or a meal. It should permeate our personal interactions as well. How can you welcome others into conversations about spiritual topics in a way that demonstrates you truly want to understand their point of view before offering your own?

4. Read Matthew 25:35-36. How did Jesus describe true hospitality?

LifeLine

Biblical hospitality is a reflection of a welcoming heart,
not a picture-perfect home.

OUTLIVING YOUR LIFE

Men and women don't live very long;
like wildflowers they spring up and blossom,
But a storm snuffs them out just as quickly,
leaving nothing to show they were here.
GOD's love, though, is ever and always,
eternally present to all who fear him,
Making everything right for them and their children
as they follow his Covenant ways
and remember to do whatever he said.

PSALM 103:15-18, MSG

How DO THE FIRST FOUR LINES of this Scripture passage make you feel? Do they invoke renewed energy, inspiring you to make the most of the few years we're given, or is it depressing that the psalmist compares our lives to flowers that bloom only for a short season? If you're a follower of Christ, you have the assurance of eternal life, but it's natural to want to make a difference on this side of eternity as well.

That's what Jimma did.

The message arrived late one afternoon. The former professor I and hundreds of other alumni called Jimma was gone. I had lost a father once before, and this news brought a familiar sorrow.

What was it about the death of this educator that caused waves of grief to rock the internet? Classmates who hadn't been in touch for years reached for one another's hearts across the internet, offering personal memories as if they were siblings remembering a beloved father. As I read the tributes online, I realized that the intentionality and love with which Jimma had lived his life revealed a profound part of his Father's heart.

He knew us. He loved us. He named us. Jimma gave each of his students a unique nickname. Mine was Mahdia—some derivation of my childhood nickname, Marji. A Facebook thread wove its way through social media with dozens of comments from former classmates, reminiscing about the names they had received. There is something special about being known and loved in a way personal to each individual. Perhaps it's a forerunner to what God promises us:

> I will give to each one [who believes] a white stone, and
> on the stone will be engraved a new name *that no one*
> *understands except the one who receives it.*[1]

Years after graduation, I returned to campus for a surprise sixty-fifth birthday party for Jimma. As his former students waited their turns to greet him, I was astonished to hear Jimma inquire after their spouses and children by name. When it was my turn for a hug, he didn't miss a beat. "Mahdia! How is Mike?" he inquired eagerly. "And Adam, Amber, and Jordan?"

Later at their home, I asked Jimma's wife, June, how her husband could possibly remember hundreds of his former students as well as the names of their families. June looked surprised. "He prays for you all," she said simply.

The intimacy and deep care of consistently praying for others and loving those they love is a lasting gift that resonates deeply in another's life. It speaks far beyond the present moment.

He discussed us with God. Jimma and June lived well over a mile from campus. Fair weather or foul, he walked to school, and as he did, he talked to God about his kids—his own sons as well as his expanding tribe of students, past and present. Jimma never stopped reminding his Father of our needs. His intercession was like that of the apostle Paul, who wrote,

> God knows how often I pray for you. Day and night I bring
> you and your needs in prayer to God.[2]

Nearly fifteen years after my last class with Jimma, our two-year-old son was admitted to Boston Children's Hospital for lifesaving surgery. Those were pre–cell phone days. It was nearly impossible for anyone to reach us in the waiting room where Mike and I were pacing. But someone did.

A beckoning hand from a nurse. A call to the pay phone on the wall. A familiar voice. "June and I are praying for Jordan, and we couldn't wait to hear . . . how is he?" That phone call came thirty years ago, but I still recall how astonished we were that my old professor had tracked us down.

Is there someone waiting to hear from you today? From me?

He believed in us when we didn't believe in ourselves. When I initially auditioned for the drama workout group in college—a prerequisite for being cast in productions—I was thrilled and terrified to be accepted. I didn't think I had what it took to be an actor. I was too introverted, too conventional. My classmates had big personalities, while mine paled in comparison. They were chocolate, pistachio, tutti-frutti. I was vanilla.

Jimma never expected me to be anything other than who I was, yet he pushed me fiercely to become more than I ever thought I could be. He rebuked me when I deserved it. He accepted me without condition. I can hear his voice in Paul's words to his loved ones in Philippi:

> My dear brothers and sisters, stay true to the Lord. I love you and long to see you . . . for you are my joy and the crown I receive for my work.[3]

A former classmate spoke for all of us when he commented, "How lucky we are that someone so holy, human, and loving, so disciplining, real, and truthful, so candid and supportive was a part of our lives. We were all special to him. That love changed the trajectory of our lives."[4]

Do you want to outlive your life? You don't have to be a parent, coach, or teacher like Jimma. Find younger people and get to know them. Love them. Help them discover their unique purpose. Discuss them with God.

And never stop believing in them, even when they don't believe in themselves.

Points of Connection

1. Psalm 103:15-18 speaks plainly of the transitory nature of life. Other than ashes in an urn or bones in a box, nothing will remain of our physical presence here. Most of us won't be an

architect leaving behind completed buildings or a physician leaving patients whose lives have been saved. What are some unique ways you can permanently impact the world you will leave behind?

2. In addition to children you might be privileged to raise, coach, or teach, whose life can you touch in ways that will outlive your own? How can you use your time to leave a legacy of love and service in the years to come?

3. Read today's Scripture passages again. How do the best mentors point us toward the everlasting love of our heavenly Father?

LifeLine

Outliving your life is about building into others to equip them
for what they'll someday do.

PART IV

The God of Your Journey

Remember, merciful Jesus, that I am the cause of Your journey.

TRANSLATION OF A LINE FROM MOZART'S *Requiem*

HAVE YOU EVER TAKEN YOUR EYES off a child for a moment or two, only for them to become lost? Whether the separation lasts minutes, hours, or longer, the horror of their disappearance time-stamps your brain with trauma.

One heart-stopping day nearly thirty years ago, our youngest son, Jordan, wandered away from our family while we were listening to historic interpreters at Plimoth Plantation in Massachusetts. Clutching the hands of our older children, Mike and I ran through the site, screaming Jordan's name until we found him safely in the care of an employee near the entrance gate. I still have nightmares about the incident.

So my sympathies are fully with Mary, mother of Jesus, for her frantic response after becoming separated from her oldest child for a full three days. Jesus' family had joined a caravan of other travelers returning to Nazareth after celebrating the Passover in Jerusalem.[1] When Mary didn't see her überresponsible firstborn among their relatives and friends, she may have assumed he was assisting other families. (Something tells me that came naturally to Jesus, even at twelve.) But when he was nowhere to be found, Mary and Joseph hurried back to Jerusalem and searched for him everywhere, only to finally locate him in the inner courtyard of the Temple, listening and asking questions of the teachers.

We can relate to Mary's stern questioning, born out of days of stomach-churning fear: "Son, why have you treated us like this? Your father and I have been anxiously searching for you." What strikes me about the account, though, is that the separation was not on Jesus' part. Scripture tells us that while Jesus was still in Jerusalem, the group left for home, "thinking he was in their company." Jesus' human family left him behind, and they traveled on thinking they were mindful of him when they were not. Jesus did not leave them. They were the ones who left him.

How powerfully convicting that passage has become to me! I know Jesus, love him, and fully intend to stay close to him every day. But how often do I travel on my oblivious little way, thinking I'm being mindful of him, when I'm not?

Acknowledged or not, the God of our journey is present with us at all times, in all ways, in all circumstances. Our first parents, Adam and Eve, were aware of God's presence walking with them in the Garden. It was their sinful actions that caused the terrible separation theologians speak of as "the Fall." Even after that, God makes a promise to his people: "I will walk among you and be your God, and you will be my people."[2] Then he did just that, coming to Earth in the person of Jesus. As Apollo 15 astronaut Jim Irwin once said, "God walking on the Earth is more important than man walking on the moon."[3]

God is not simply an aspect of our lives but rather the one who is in and over all things. Our Alpha and Omega. The beginning and the end of our journeys on this side of eternity. And he sent his only Son to take on our flesh and blood and move into the neighborhood.[4] He came not only as Savior but as Friend. We are the cause of his journey from heaven to earth. We can walk the road of our lives with confidence because of the one who came to walk with us. Let's learn how to find the God of our journey in every part of what we do.

HEY, THEOPHILUS! BECOMING A FRIEND OF GOD

[Jesus said,] "You are my friends when you do the things I command
you. I'm no longer calling you servants because servants don't understand
what their master is thinking and planning. No, I've named you friends
because I've let you in on everything I've heard from the Father."

JOHN 15:14-15, MSG

THIS WEEK, I RECEIVED AN INVITATION to a Galentine's luncheon hosted by a woman who lives nearby. Having just relocated this past year, I've struggled with the loneliness of starting over and making new friends. To be invited to a social gathering gives me hope that I have a place here after all. Someone knows my name. Woo-hoo!

Invitations are at the heart of social networks, too. Who doesn't want to be included, to have our presence desired at an event? We issue friend requests or accept them. We follow, post, and tweet to engage with those we know or would like to know. We're invited to watch live events taking place thousands of miles away. At the center of it all is the desire to experience community, to have friends.

The most important invitation in history is at the heart of the gospel: *Whoever believes will have eternal life.* Ask someone to quote a Scripture reference, and you'll probably hear John 3:16. Athletes have painted it on their foreheads. The passage has been preached with passion from a million pulpits. It's an invitation not only to live forever but to enter a life-changing relationship.

To be a friend of God.

Both the Gospel of Luke and the book of Acts are addressed to a man named Theophilus, which means "friend of God." Does it sound arrogant, even irreverent, to call God "friend"? He's not a buddy or boyfriend. The Creator of the universe is someone we address as Father, or by the affectionate *Abba*.[1] But a parent's love includes discipline, training, and rebuke, actions that don't characterize most friendships. Can God really be friend as well as Father?

Jesus said that those who had seen him had seen his Father.[2] He took on flesh to come to our poor planet and experience our limitations and temptations, pledging to never leave us.[3] Someone who enters your world, identifies with you, and promises never to leave you alone is one awesome friend.

What qualifies us to be considered friends of God? Let's think about some of the people God called friends in Scripture. There's Abraham, for one.[4] And David was famously called a man after God's own heart.[5] Yet Abraham lied about his own wife and had sex with her servant, while David one-upped that by not only sleeping with another man's wife but ensuring that Bathsheba's husband would meet an untimely death. So, yeah, that rules out moral superiority or exemplary performance as a friendship qualification.

Jesus had a wide circle of friends during his public years of ministry: the multitudes, the seventy-two,[6] the twelve disciples, and the three in his most trusted inner circle: Peter, James, and John. What encourages me the most, though, are his recorded friendships with women.

Sisters Mary and Martha of Bethany used the phrase "dear friend" to describe their brother's relationship (and theirs) with Jesus.[7] He gave his devoted follower Mary Magdalene the privilege of being the first person to bear witness to his resurrection.[8] For a Jewish rabbi to even speak to a woman outside of his family circle ran counter to culture, but that's exactly what Jesus was. Radically countercultural.

The kind of friend I want and desperately need.

The Bible is clear about the only requirements for friendship with God: Faith followed by obedience. The apostle Paul writes, "Therefore, since we have been made right in God's sight by faith, we have peace with God because of what Jesus Christ our Lord has done for us. Because of our faith, Christ has brought us into this place of undeserved privilege where we now stand, and we confidently and joyfully look forward to sharing God's glory."[9]

And Jesus put it plainly: "You are my friends when you do the things I command you. I'm no longer calling you servants because servants don't understand what their master is thinking and planning. No, I've named you friends because I've let you in on everything I've heard from the Father."[10]

Jesus is the only friend who can give us true peace with God. He's the one who invites us into this intimate relationship: access by faith into grace. As his friends, we get the privilege of following where he leads. And with peace and privilege comes the lasting promise that we'll be perfected at the last day.

If you've never accepted his invitation to enter his family, he may be speaking to you right now: "Look! I stand at the door and knock. If you hear my voice and open the door, I will come in, and we will share a meal together as friends."[11]

It's what friends do.

And I guarantee you, Theophilus, this one will change your life.

Points of Connection

1. What surprises you most about the idea of God being your friend? Does anything trouble you about this concept?

2. Read Mark 6:30-46, focusing on Jesus' invitation to the disciples in verse 31. What does this reveal about Jesus' care for them as his friends? Can you imagine Jesus issuing this same invitation to you today? What might Jesus see that you need most when you're surrounded by so many pressing concerns?

3. Oswald Chambers once wrote, "There is only one relationship that matters, and that is your personal relationship to a personal Redeemer and Lord. Let everything else go, but maintain that at all costs, and God will fulfill His purpose through your life. One life may be of priceless value to God's purposes, and yours may be that life."[12] How does this statement challenge you to reconsider personal priorities?

Life Line

When we enter God's family, we become his friends. Saving the world is his job; ours is to do as he directs.

SANCTUARY

We who have fled to him for refuge can have great confidence as we hold to the hope that lies before us. This hope is a strong and trustworthy anchor for our souls. It leads us through the curtain into God's inner sanctuary.

HEBREWS 6:18-19, NLT

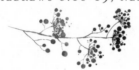

RECENTLY, MY HUSBAND AND I decided to sublet some property. He swept out the rental unit and gave it a fresh coat of white paint, and it was ready for occupancy.

Within forty-eight hours, a young couple had checked it out, and the next day we were delighted to observe them moving in. We stood on our sun porch, cameras clicking like proud parents as we watched them furnish their nest. A literal one.

To some, our new tenants' home is a simple steepled birdhouse, a nest where they can nurture their young, but we intend it as something more—a sanctuary. A place of protection against predators and a shelter from storms.

I love the concept of sanctuary and instinctively seek it wherever I go. When Mike and I were first married, I held down a stressful corporate job in downtown Boston. Even when nature didn't demand it, I'd sometimes escape to the restroom, latch the door, and slump against it for a few minutes, grateful for a few moments of peace and quiet.

Throughout our decades of marriage, Mike and I have made our home available as a sanctuary for people as well as wildlife. A mom and her four teens stayed with us one special summer when they were between homes. College students who needed respite from dorm life knew they were welcome to use our home as a study hall. Preteen friends of our children whose family was in crisis came for a long weekend and stayed for five years.

New churches generally label large gathering spaces as worship centers rather than sanctuaries, but whatever you call the space where we gather together, we need it. When we were in the pastorate and I no longer had young children to wrangle, I was grateful to be able to attend multiple services in the same morning. The first service filled my cup and the second topped it off.

At the end of a long week crowded with commitments, corporate worship allows recalibration. With the focus off self, we see God instead. Our hands and hearts move heavenward. We process finite experiences in the presence of an infinite God.

You don't have to enter a church to find sanctuary. Susanna Wesley, mother of John and Charles and a passel of other children, threw her apron over her head when she needed private time with her Creator.

Ruth Bell Graham often parented their five children solo when her evangelist-husband, Billy, was traveling. Ruth kept her Bible open on the table so she could snatch passages to feed her soul while she was feeding her kids.[1]

Jonathan Edwards, a student of the natural world as well as theology, would venture out on horseback to find sanctuary. When he returned home, his wife, Sarah, would carefully unpin the sermon notes he had scribbled and stuck to his greatcoat.

If your life is crammed with people, activities, and commitments (as mine has always been), I'm praying you'll seek sanctuary, too—frequent times of solitude when you can turn your heart toward your heavenly Home.

Jesus regularly took time away from the crowds to seek communion with his Father. His public ministry lasted only three years. It would be understandable if he had foregone rest. He had an eternity to spend with God. But he needed that consistent time alone with his Father. And so do we.

Our chickadee tenants seem to appreciate their new church-home. "Baptist birds!" Mike declared cheerfully. "Or maybe they've been church-hopping for a while and decided to settle where they knew they'd be welcome."

No matter. Their one-foot-square apartment in the sky is a sanctuary to them.

Whether your world is marvelously wide at present or as confined as that of our tenants, you can find sanctuary too.

Right here. Right now.

Points of Connection

1. There are many scriptural references to Jesus' desire for times of solitude and sanctuary with his Father. Take time to consider these key passages: Matthew 14:23; Mark 1:35; Mark 14:32; Luke 6:12-13; John 7:10. How does reflecting on Jesus' priorities help reorder your own?

2. Where are places in your life that have been a sanctuary for you? What did they have in common?

3. In what ways can you build space into the rhythm of your days to create times of silence and solitude to recalibrate your life before God?

LifeLine

Whether you find sanctuary in a church building, a park, or your own backyard, make time to be alone with God.

THE FRAGRANCE OF FAITH

[Jesus said,] "Let me tell you why you are here. You're here to be salt-seasoning that brings out the God-flavors of this earth. If you lose your saltiness, how will people taste godliness? You've lost your usefulness and will end up in the garbage."

MATTHEW 5:13, MSG

I SAT IN A SALT CAVE ON SUNDAY.

No, not the kind that is springing up in day spas[1] around the country. I hadn't even heard of them until a discount offer for "salt cave sessions" popped up in my inbox from a popular group-purchasing site. The tempting pitch ran something like this:

Ageless Day Spa & Salt Cave surrounds patrons with a nourishing antiaging regimen replete with sustentative body regimens and beautifying spa treatments. It's hard to make a case for *pro*-aging, but what under God's blue heaven is a "sustentative" body regimen?

Enveloped by the dim light and sea sounds filling the salt cave, beach chairs nestle physiques while patrons savor the pure air. Ah, now they're reeling me in. Dim light, sea sounds, and pure air reminds me of Cape Cod. But I've never met a beach chair yet that nestled my physique.

Crafted from Himalayan salt, the cave infuses the atmosphere with constitution-enhancing minerals, body-balancing ions, and the scent of potato chips in bloom. Never mind the minerals that promise to enhance my maturing constitution. Forget the ions that will balance this sagging body. They had me at the scented potato chips.

But before I hit the "Buy Now" button, I realized I already benefit from salt cave sessions every week.

Each Sunday morning, I perch on a pew, surrounded by people with whom I'm in community. People who enhance the flavor of my life as well as the lives of so many others. People who intentionally engage the culture not only to preserve it but to serve it.

In our post-truth culture, this saltiness is increasingly unacceptable. Polls continue to produce statistics claiming that those without religious affiliation, the "nones," are the fastest-growing "religious group" today.[2] A generation of young adults raised in the church is moving away from its influence, convinced that Christians don't represent the values most important to them.

The preservative and medicinal properties of salt are well known. But in a culture that increasingly marginalizes the importance of faith, how can we demonstrate a genuine concern for others in the ways Christ intended?

In the Kalahari Desert region of southern Africa, residents use salt in a unique way to locate water. "Monkeys in this desert region always know where to find water, but they are very careful not to show humans its location. People will trap a monkey and feed it salt until it is extremely thirsty. When released, the monkey runs straight to the water source, unaware it is being followed."[3] As followers of Christ, our challenge is to make others thirsty for the living water that is Jesus.[4]

Just as our bodies require sodium chloride to sustain life, we need the body of Christ. When Jesus told his followers, "You are the salt of the earth,"[5] he meant it. It's time for us to stop focusing so much of our energies on peripheral stuff and instead live in such love and generosity of spirit that others become thirsty for that which spiritually hydrates us.

The taste and fragrance of faith. It's a little like potato chips in bloom.

Points of Connection

1. As a substance, salt may seem homogenous, but sodium chloride is formulated in dozens of varieties. Browse the aisles of a specialty store, and you'll find rose-colored salt mined in the Himalayas, charcoal flakes from the Mediterranean region, and black Hiwa Kai or red Alaea from the Hawaiian Islands. How might the diverse nature of salt encourage you to live out Jesus' mandate found in Matthew 5:13?

2. Salt is never consumed by itself. When we come on too strong, we turn others away. Colossians 4:6 reminds us to let our conversation "be always full of grace, seasoned with salt, so that [we] may know how to answer everyone." How can this instruction help us handle potentially divisive conversations?

3. By their very nature, salt crystals are tiny and often invisible, but it's obvious when they're lacking. If you moved or your church left the area, would your influence disappear as well? What are some ways you can connect with your surrounding community to make a lasting impact?

LifeLine

Seasoning draws attention to the food it enhances, not itself.
Serve others in a way that demonstrates your love for every kind of
person Jesus loves.

GOD SO LOVED THE WORLD. DO WE?

Learn to do good.
Seek justice.
Help the oppressed.
Defend the cause of orphans.
Fight for the rights of widows.

ISAIAH 1:17, NLT

THAT FAMILY . . . you know them too. The impoverished teenage mom, her older husband, and the child (definitely not his) they covenanted to raise together. They were scraping by in their home country when the news came. No glad tidings of great joy this time. It was shocking, horrific, the kind that startles you awake with sweat glazing your brow, despite the arid Middle Eastern climate.

The warning arrived wrapped in darkness, whispered into the ears of a working-class man. There was no mistaking the message.

Get up. Take the child. Get out. Go. NOW.

To stay would mean certain death—if not for the parents, then certainly for the child.

So they took what little they could carry, maybe the bit of gold they'd been gifted and spices for sacrifice. They crossed the border, their status assured not by the local authorities but by the one who sent them. A family under orders.

Who would be willing to help them on the other side? In their new country, their story would sound sketchy at best and paranoid at worst. (The king reportedly wanted to murder their son. Seriously?) They could not speak the local language. Who would hire a Judean carpenter to work in their homes or his young wife to watch their children? The Bible is silent on that part of their story.

But ours are still being written. And the Bible is not silent on how the people of God are to respond to those who are in need in our day, just as Jesus and his earthly family were in theirs.

Early in 2018, top evangelical leaders from all fifty states signed an open letter to the US president and members of Congress, urging action to help vulnerable immigrants. The letter cited "the dramatic reduction in arrivals of refugees to the United States, [with the government] on track to admit the lowest number of refugees since the formalization of the US Refugee Resettlement Program in 1980."[1] The United States Commission on International Religious Freedom expressed deep concern at reports that the federal government might reduce refugee arrivals in fiscal year 2020 to zero.[2]

Scripture is clear that followers of Christ must work toward justice for the most vulnerable among us. This means giving a voice to the unborn, the poor, and the marginalized in all corners of society, including refugees and those persecuted for their faith. If we remain silent, who will speak for them? The US Constitution opens with the famous words "We the People," but the Bible speaks of "We, his people."[3] We're under orders too.

In an increasingly secular culture, people of faith are castigated for offering thoughts and prayers in the wake of a natural disaster or mass shooting. Those who dismiss prayer as futile fail to recognize that intercession is the most powerful force in the universe. John Wesley famously said that God will do nothing but in response to prayer.

Prayer is not an excuse for passivity, though. Rather, it is a meeting with the King of justice to seek his intervention and to align ourselves with his ways and his will. Prayer is not our only response to injustice, but it informs our entire response to justice.[4]

As we pray, the Holy Spirit works to direct our response toward compassionate action. The Christian humanitarian organization Samaritan's Purse stocks supplies in warehouses throughout the world, in order to respond at a moment's notice when disaster strikes. World Relief advocates on behalf of refugees and displaced persons. The Voice of the Martyrs reminds us not to forget those persecuted for their faith. Whether we join forces with an organization or launch our own initiatives, we need to love the same people God loves: all people.

Throughout history, women of faith have been at the forefront of seeking justice for the poor, the oppressed, and those victimized by cultural practices that legitimize abuse. Deborah was a highly respected, long-serving judge in ancient Israel. Sojourner Truth, born into slavery in the early nineteenth century, won her freedom and traveled widely, preaching the gospel while seeking to abolish slavery. Missionary Amy Carmichael rescued hundreds of children sold into temple prostitution in India.

Jesus taught his followers that whatever we do for the least of these, we also do for him.[5] Pastor and author Scott Sauls places the imperative to befriend strangers and refugees in its biblical context:

[True believers] will have been the ones who—in contributing to the welcome of alien and stranger, in

participating in care for the least of these, in doing
something big or small to provide food for the hungry and a
drink for the thirsty and shelter for those without a home—
will have welcomed King Jesus himself.[6]

God is the Redeemer of the world, but he chooses to work
through his people to demonstrate divine love and compassion.
We can pray for those in need, give financially, or open our homes,
hearts, and hands to provide for others. Or all of the above!

Points of Connection

1. Read Acts 1:8. What do you think it means to be God's
   witnesses "in Jerusalem, and in all Judea and Samaria, and to
   the ends of the earth"? Does serving as a witness go beyond
   sharing the Good News of salvation through faith? How can
   we put hands and feet to our testimony?

2. Scott Sauls has said that "the narrow path of Jesus demands the
   widest embrace."[7] Consider Luke 15:1-7, 11-32. What were
   some of the ways in which Jesus reached out to those outside
   the conventional boundaries of religion and society? How can
   we do the same?

LifeLine

We love the world because God loved it first.

DO I LOVE TO TELL THE STORY?

As she listened with intensity to what was being said,
the Master gave her a trusting heart—
and she believed!

ACTS 16:14, MSG

IF THERE WERE AWARDS for Kitchen Evangelists, I'd be a contender.

For sixteen years of our marriage, we lived in a century-old home in the Midwest that had "potential" when we bought it. All the rooms needed work, but none more so than the kitchen—a tiny galley with beat-up white laminate cabinets and mirrored backsplashes (to ensure messes were magnified). It was so small, you couldn't turn around when the dishwasher door was open.

With kids in college and minimal funds for renovation, we lived with that kitchen for years until a miracle happened—a family in our neighborhood gave us their old cherry cabinetry when they remodeled. Keith, a gifted craftsman we dubbed our kitchen cardiologist, transformed the heart of our home by pushing out a wall and retrofitting the old cabinets into our expanded space. When

visitors commented on our beautiful new kitchen, I loved to tell
the story of its spectacular transformation.

So why am I practically mute when it comes to sharing my
story of spiritual transformation?

Generations of Christians have sung a Civil War–era hymn that
joyfully expresses our desire to share our faith:

> *I love to tell the story*
> *of unseen things above,*
> *of Jesus and his glory,*
> *of Jesus and his love.*
> *I love to tell the story,*
> *because I know 'tis true;*
> *it satisfies my longings*
> *as nothing else could do.*[1]

But is that true? Do we really "love to tell the story"?

Recent studies indicate that half of millennial Christians, those
born roughly in the 1980s and 1990s, say it's wrong to evangelize.[2]
They are enthusiastic about Jesus but not necessarily about the
older evangelism approaches. Our prevailing Western culture dis-
courages speaking out about others' personal choices, including
their spiritual faith or lack of it. Despite the confidence we have
from Scripture, how can we tell others that Jesus is the only way to
God[3] without seeming to make a value judgment that smacks of
exclusivity?

It's not only millennials who struggle with this. It's rare to find
American believers willing to hand out tracts or go door-to-door
to present the gospel to strangers. (What if they think we're "one of
them"?) In the past, tens of thousands attended evangelistic crusades,

but both the name and the practice have fallen out of favor. Revival services take place primarily in rural pockets of the Bible Belt. Even global programs designed to provide space for exploring questions of faith struggle to gain a hearing in many areas.

What I've observed with younger friends is that many do express a genuine desire to share their faith with others, albeit in ways that are organic and within the context of a relationship where they know the other person feels cared for regardless of differences. They are not resistant to evangelism but rather to what feels like inauthenticity or "turning people into a project." The postmodern context in contemporary culture prioritizes relationship, and if that's not present, we won't get a hearing for conversations about spiritual matters. But even as we wrestle with the right *way* to share our faith, let's not forget that each person we know has a profound need to hear the grace-filled gospel story of redemption.

As I write, the three largest Christian denominational bodies in the United States have come under the media spotlight for issues revolving around clergy sexual abuse, hierarchical cover-ups, and questions of sexual ethics. Commenting on the stories in the news, my own pastor challenged our congregation to remember the central tenets of our faith, pointing out that many twenty-first-century churches are performing more funerals these days than baptisms.

While it's imperative for the church to authentically confront issues of morality and social justice, it's too easy to overlook the fact that Scripture teaches that those without a personal relationship with Jesus are bound for a Christless eternity.[4] I am preaching to myself here, friends, not pointing a finger at anyone else. I travel often by plane, but do I seize the opportunity to respectfully speak with my seatmates about my hope in Jesus? Am I actively involved in organizations[5] designed to help believers share their faith winsomely? Do I support friends who have emotional or physical needs but fail to address their spiritual ones?

And, given the dynamics of our postmodern culture, how do I build relationships with eternity in mind? How do I love people without turning them into projects? How do I remain sensitive to the Spirit so that I can be both courageous and discerning when it comes to evangelism? And how do I keep the relationship priority from becoming an excuse to not share my faith?

These are difficult questions in a postmodern, secular age, but they're critically important. Most of us are happy to share bargain buys, our own resources, or fun experiences with our friends, yet we often shy away from speaking about the most important decision of all: where we will spend eternity.

Jesus put it this way: "What do you benefit if you gain the whole world but lose your own soul? Is anything worth more than your soul?"[6]

I loved being a Kitchen Evangelist, repeatedly telling the story of the transformation of the heart of our home. And when it comes to the heart of the matter, the renovation of someone's soul, how can I remain silent?

How can any of us?

Points of Connection

1. There are other ways to share the reality of our faith besides handing out tracts or conducting door-to-door evangelism. Methods that were effective in previous generations often turn people away today. I have used drama to convey the reality of my life with Jesus and to share the lives of great women of the faith. My friend Lea paints oils depicting God's creation and

displays them in her senior community. Teams from my church demonstrate God's love by working together to build homes and provide daily meals for the underserved in our community. My teenage buddy Sarah sports temporary Scripture tattoos on her arms and has engaged friends in conversation about them. In what ways can you share your faith that are consistent with your giftedness and personality?

2. Read the story of Lydia in Acts 16:13-15. What are some of the ways God worked in and through women in the early church to further the spread of the Good News of the gospel? Can you reimagine their efforts in our contemporary culture?

Life Line

Sharing the free gift of faith in Jesus Christ is an act of great love.

THE PARADOX OF UNANSWERED PRAYER

[Jesus said,] "The world is full of so-called prayer warriors who are prayer-ignorant. They're full of formulas and programs and advice, peddling techniques for getting what you want from God. Don't fall for that nonsense. This is your Father you are dealing with, and he knows better than you what you need."

MATTHEW 6:7-8, MSG

IT WAS A CHANCE ENCOUNTER. And then again, maybe not.

Some years back, my husband and I were vacationing in the Smokies. One night, we left our cabin to scout out a place for dinner in a nearby town we'd never visited before.

Noticing a large crowd downtown, we discovered a street dance taking place near the county courthouse. A bluegrass band played while adults and kids of all ages followed the directions of a caller. Intrigued, we plopped down on the grass to watch, only to have a young couple nearby offer us their lawn chairs.

We exchanged first names, chatting casually while watching the dancing. Amy was tall, slender, and dusky blonde; she and her husband, Billy Joe, were local, while we lived hundreds of miles north. But when twilight fell over the mountains and our new friends packed up to leave, Amy blurted out, "Hey, I know we just met, but would you pray for us? Billy and I have been trying for years to have a baby, and there's nothing the doctors can do. You seem like praying people. Would y'all remember us?"

Touched, we promised we would. Infertility is not only agonizing but all too common. At any one time we've known several couples hoping for a child just as Amy and Billy were. As we prayed for each family in the years ahead, we prayed for this young North Carolina couple too.

Did we believe God could give them a child? We sure did. Did we believe he would? That's where faith falters.

In Scripture, we're told to ask for what we need and also what our hearts desire.[1] It's our part of the partnership in how God chooses to work in the world. But are we guaranteed an answer?

Some say so. It's like a spiritual traffic signal, they claim. You might get God's green light, or a red that's a clear no, or maybe even a yellow indicating "wait." But the answer will come. And when the light of eternity illuminates all our questions, our need for answers will fade away. I believe that. I do.

But sometimes there's no signal that God has heard us. Months pass, years maybe, and the situation remains unchanged. Is he saying, "Hold on here; the answer's on its way," or does the silence indicate that our petition has been denied?

In the book of Acts, the believers praying fervently for the incarcerated apostle Peter rejoice when God uses miraculous means to free him from prison.[2] Yet in that same passage, we learn the apostle James has been executed.

Did God love Peter more than he did James? Did the believers praying for Peter have more faith than those interceding for James?

Scripture is clear that our Creator loves each of us equally.[3] There's nothing we can do to make him love us more or less. And while faith is crucially important in the life of the believer—a sign of our trust in God's ultimate will for our lives—prayers are not answered according to some divine formula calculated by the abundance or lack of faith.[4]

If I claim to have the definitive answer to a conundrum that has perplexed God's people since time began, you might as well toss this book into the trash. If I could tell you something new that speaks with certainty about the paradoxical problems of pain, suffering, and unanswered prayer, you should brand me a heretic. Because faith is exactly that: faith. The certainty of things not seen.[5] Of answers shrouded in divine mystery that may not be visible this side of eternity.

I've lost my parents and some of my closest friends to terminal illnesses. I've begged God to vindicate loved ones who were victims of false accusations, only to have the situations drag on for years. At times, I've felt like the psalmist who lamented, "Why, LORD, do you reject me and hide your face from me?"[6]

But still I pray. Because I must. Because God's Word tells me to. Because along with the anguish of loss, I've also experienced the wild joy of God's glorious YES.

After my husband, mom, and I relocated to the Smokies this past year, we discovered that the residents of our new hometown are still square-dancing in the streets on summer nights.

On the last night of the season, as the shadow of Cold Mountain lengthened over the dancers, I spotted a tall young woman with hair like ripened wheat. *Amy.* Though several years had passed, her face had never left my mind, even as her quiet petition had never left my prayers.

The crowd was dispersing, but I pushed my way through, hoping to speak with her. I wanted her to know these strangers had not forgotten her request.

Then she turned, stooped, and opened her arms wide to scoop up a tiny towheaded boy toddling toward her, his face wreathed in smiles, hers in welcome.

I had my answer. And I went home dancing.

Points of Connection

1. What are some deep concerns you've carried in prayer without yet receiving an answer? Record them in a prayer journal with today's date, noting on the December page of your calendar to review them at year's end. You may well be amazed at how answers have come in ways you never expected.

2. Lots of Scripture passages on prayer are referenced in today's reading. As time permits, read Psalms 37:4; 88:14; 91:15; and Jeremiah 31:3 in the Old Testament. And read Matthew 7:7-8; Luke 11:9; John 3:16; 15:7; Romans 1:17; 5:8; and Hebrews 11:1 in the New. The Bible was never meant to be read one verse at a time but rather as a whole. What new insights do you see when you consider the broad view of biblical teaching on intercession?

Life Line

The power in prayer is not in the words themselves or in the ones who pray but rather in the one who hears us. Even when you can't see him at work, you can trust his loving and good intentions toward you.

PAPERWHITES AND PRAYER

I'm sure now I'll see God's goodness
in the exuberant earth.
Stay with GOD!
Take heart. Don't quit.
I'll say it again:
Stay with GOD.

PSALM 27:13-14, MSG

I BOUGHT THEM AT ONE OF THOSE BIG-BOX STORES a couple weeks before Christmas: two small square containers sporting optimistic photographs of paperwhite flowers. Spring in a box for only five dollars. When I dumped them out, the contents were unimpressive: cheap plastic pots, a meager amount of potting soil, and a few dead-looking bulbs.

Here goes nothing, I muttered as I filled the containers, inserted the bulbs, and shoved the pots into a southeastern window. In the rush of work, travel, and Christmas preparations, I had little time to tend them. My eyes skittered over them while washing dishes, too busy to notice whether the ugly bulbs were pushing tentative green shoots from their windowsill bed. After a while, I failed to see them at all.

It felt depressingly like my life in that season. Working full-time, taking grad classes, and tending to the needs of our family as well as our church took every moment I had and plenty I didn't. But my frenzied efforts, especially in the gray gloom of Chicago midwinter, often seemed as opaque as those brown bulbs—little to show for late nights and constant activity.

Perhaps you're staring at this page right now, wondering about your own life. You're taking classes, but to what end? You have a job, but is it a vocation or does it just pay the bills? You're investing all your daytime hours—and maybe nighttime, too—wrangling kiddos or caring for an ailing spouse or aging parent. Tomorrow you'll do it all over again.

When will you see results? Does anyone really notice or appreciate how hard you're trying? What if you're giving all you've got, only to discover it still isn't enough?

The first followers of Jesus experienced these same frustrations. His disciples had the unprecedented privilege of walking with him daily and witnessing countless miracles, both physical and spiritual, yet they longed to know what it all meant. Would Jesus overthrow the government and free them from Roman oppression? Would he take them all with him when he returned to his Father? How would the story end?

On the night he was betrayed, Jesus washed the disciples' feet. When he came to Simon Peter, Peter protested in confusion. Shouldn't Jesus be about more significant tasks? They had so little time. What was his master doing?

Jesus replied, "You don't understand now what I am doing, but someday you will."[1]

You don't understand.

No, Lord, I don't. I've worked and I've prayed and I've cried out to you, but it seems there's so little to show for my efforts. Those students I discipled—did all those hours we spent together produce any lasting fruit?

My family. Do they remember the meals I cooked, the activities I planned, the opportunities I set aside to give most of my time to them instead? Did it make a difference?

The church I served for so many years. I worked on committees, made calls, taught lessons, served in the nursery. I wanted to take that which came to me as seed and see it blossom in the lives of others. But in the end, did all those hours count for anything? Did I waste my life when I could have been pursuing other things?

You're right that I don't understand, Lord. I see what could have been, but I'm stuck in what is. There's a valley in between that I can't cross.

It's January in my soul, overcast and gray. But as I came in after church this morning and paused, an unfamiliar fragrance drew my eyes to the southeastern window.

The paperwhites. Almost overnight, they've burst into bloom, their sturdy apple-green stalks thrusting up masses of fragrant blooms like tiny stars set against the gunmetal sky. The dun-colored bulbs that were dormant have burst into life.

You did the planting. Leave the outcome to me.

I close my eyes and breathe deeply, shoulders back, body relaxing into the sanctuary of home. The paperwhites have bloomed, and as I inhale their sweetness, I exhale a prayer.

Points of Connection

1. In what parts of your life right now do you long to see a positive outcome? Do you have a relationship that's tenuous,

a difficult employment situation, or an unsettling medical diagnosis? How can Jesus' words to Peter become his reassurance to you today?

2. Look at the following passages: Psalms 13:5; 44:4-8; Hebrews 10:36; James 5:7. How do these verses teach us to leave the outcome to God?

3. Scripture promises God is continually present with his people. Picture him sitting beside you right now. What would you say to him about the situations in your life that appear dormant?

Life Line

God lives in the gap between what could have been and what is.

Leave the outcome to him.

WHAT WAS I THINKING?

The kind of sorrow God wants us to experience leads us away from sin and results in salvation. There's no regret for that kind of sorrow.

2 CORINTHIANS 7:10, NLT

AFTER FIFTEEN YEARS IN OUR HOME, we finally repainted our living room. Constructed in 1917, the old girl was celebrating her centennial birthday, and it seemed only fitting to fete her with some new cosmetics. She practically preened under her fresh coat of "First Star," a soft gray like a twilight sky.

Someone—that would be me—had the bright idea back in the day to sponge-paint the front room a mottled egg-yolk yellow.

"What was I thinking?" I said to my husband as we admired the transformation. "The sponge-painting seemed like a good idea at the time."

"And it was." He shrugged. "Don't judge the decision you made then by how our tastes have changed now."

Practical man. And a wise one too.

I do that all the time—berate myself because my foresight is not as keen as my hindsight. I mentally criticize decisions I made years ago when factors balanced on a different scale. Is it perfectionism, fear of failure, or just plain insecurity that leads me to judge myself more harshly than I would anyone else? Have you done that too?

Several years ago, I had a poignant phone conversation with a young relative whose new marriage collapsed when his wife moved on to others and then moved out.

"I feel like such a failure," he said softly. "I'm so ashamed. Why didn't I see this coming?"

Silence stretched between us on the line. I could picture his handsome young face, drawn and grieving. I had never been in his situation, but I know what it's like to beat up on myself for the consequences of a past decision I never would have made if I'd known what I do now.

So I spoke of the only Truth firm enough to hold us steady when life leaves us flailing for answers. The God we love has shared many of his attributes with those he created, but one has been withheld: omniscience. God is all knowing; we are not.[1] He is not bound by time as we are.[2] He loved us enough to grant us our freedom to make choices. Sometimes those choices are mistakes, but a sovereign God permits those mistakes.

Regretting a paint color? Don't waste your time. Sorry you didn't look first before backing out of that parking space? Yep, it cost you. Embarrassed that your house went into foreclosure because you bought at the wrong time? The property didn't include a crystal ball. Deeply lamenting that the one who pledged to love you for better or worse turned out to *be* the worst? It's agonizing.

But, friend, hear me now. Yes, some of the pain we experience is self-inflicted: a product of our rebellion, impulse, or just plain foolishness. I've been there, done that. And the rest? The chaos we never saw coming because we were admiring the view in one direction while that dump truck of trouble came barreling out of a blind alley?

God is omniscient. We are not. He is faithful and just to forgive the whole mess of our sins, and to clean us up from all unrighteousness.[3] So can we forgive ourselves too?

There is disgrace in this life, yes, but there is also grace within disgrace.

The next time you're tempted to flagellate yourself for not knowing any better or thinking more clearly, lower the whip. Focus on the one whose back was bloodied with the lash of your sin. Mine too. The whole world's. By his stripes, we have been healed.[4]

Forgive yourself, friend. He already has. You did the best you could with what you knew to do at the time.

There's sheer grace in disgrace.

Points of Connection

1. In national interviews, celebrities sometimes comment that they have no regrets, because everything in their past has made them "who they are." But is it wise to live with no regrets? When is sorrow for past decisions counterproductive, and when is it healthy?

2. Read Acts 3:19-20 and 2 Corinthians 7:10. What does the Bible say about the kind of sorrow we should not regret?

3. When you know disobedience has led to life decisions causing remorse, remember that God has been through this before with his children. Read Romans 4:7-8, noting that we are called twice blessed when our sins are forgiven, covered, and

not counted against us. Confession is the only prerequisite to forgiveness. Is there anything you need to take to God today to receive the joy that awaits those who know they've been forgiven?

Life Line

God is all-knowing; we are not. Forgive yourself as God first forgave you. There is grace in disgrace.

TOO GOOD TO BE TRUE?
IT JUST MIGHT BE ANYWAY

No one's ever seen or heard anything like this,
Never so much as imagined anything quite like it—
What God has arranged for those who love him.

But you've seen and heard it because God by his Spirit
has brought it all out into the open before you.

I CORINTHIANS 2:9-10, MSG

THE UNEXPECTED KNOCK at the door. The friendly woman motioning to the candy dish on her table at the trade show or the county fair. The smiling guy with the outstretched arm and the clipboard in front of the library. Have you ever averted your eyes and turned away?

We all do it. Who has time for the pitch, the presentation, or the proselytizing?

As an assignment for a postgraduate class in spiritual formation that I audited, my professor tasked students with planning group service projects of random kindness and then analyzing the responses.

The reports were unexpected. One group of students tried to distribute granola bars, clementines, and bottled water at the local train station, only to find most commuters were reluctant to accept the freebies or ignored the givers entirely. Another task group attempted to hand out hot chocolate on a chilly November morning with the same result. A third threw a free picnic in the local park but attracted few participants.

As I listened to the class reports on how surprised the students were to have their good intentions met with suspicion, it wasn't difficult to parse the dynamics. Most of us aren't accustomed to getting something for nothing. If a stranger approaches us with a pleasant smile and a proffered treat, there must be a catch, right? If it's too good to be true, it probably is.

Except when it's not.

Do you have a proclivity to regard God this way? Do I?

I have no difficulty viewing him as the Father who loves me, the Son who saved me, and the Comforter who comes alongside me. I accept that when hard times enter my life, as they sometimes do, he can and will use them for good. Suffering gets our attention,[1] discipline stiffens our spiritual spines,[2] and sacrifice pleases God.[3]

I get that. But why is it so hard for many of us to accept that God cares not only about our holiness, but our happiness, too?

Author Randy Alcorn makes this distinction: "The wonderful news is that holiness doesn't mean abstaining from pleasure; holiness means recognizing Jesus as the source of life's greatest pleasure."[4]

Some of us have been taught that joy is sacred while happiness is secular. The former is to be desired while the latter is suspect, an illusory emotion dependent only upon what happens to us. But the scriptural record proves otherwise.

Consider the compelling story of the Shunammite woman in 2 Kings. This long-married wife of an older husband had stopped praying or even hoping for a child until God, working through the prophet Elisha, granted the secret desire of her heart in a miraculous way. Life with her cherished son was precious beyond belief—until her worst fears were realized. On a hot harvest day, the boy cried out in agony, clutched his head, and died.

The story of the agonized mother's race to find the prophet is told in detail in 2 Kings 4:8-37. The climactic moment occurs in her anguished cry in verse 28: "Did I ask you for a son, my lord? And didn't I say, 'Don't deceive me and get my hopes up'?"

If you've read the story, you know the ending. The death of the fulfilled promise would be the worst kind of deceit, were there no resurrection. *But there was.* The life of the Shunammite's son was restored.

Have you longed and prayed for something for so many years you've given up hope it will ever happen? Resignation is not always a bad thing. Acceptance often brings peace.

But hear me now: We need to stop putting our inner pessimist on the platform and handing him the microphone. I'm sick of lowering my expectations to avoid disappointment. Aren't you?

If this is where you are, know that God desires our happiness just as those of us who are parents delight in providing for our own children. Read today's verse again: "No eye has seen, no ear has heard, and no mind has imagined what God has prepared for those who love him."[5]

That child who has strayed so far away spiritually you fear she'll never return? The marriage that seems irretrievably, irrevocably broken? The medical diagnosis that speaks of endings but not beginnings?

Don't assume that since nothing appears to be happening in your situation right now, God is not at work. Let's not factor the Father out. He can do above and beyond what you can ask or imagine—not just for your holiness but for your happiness as well.

When your desired outcome seems too good to be true? It just might be true anyway.

Points of Connection

1. Think back through some milestone moments in your life when something amazing happened after you'd almost given up hope. Write them down to remind yourself of God's good heart for you. If you're doing this study with a friend, share a few examples and rejoice with each other!

2. First John 3:1 (NLT) contains a promise of great joy: "See how very much our Father loves us, for he calls us his children, and that is what we are!" How does your view of your present circumstance change when you accept that God is a loving Father who desires the best for you, his child? Read Matthew 7:9-11.

3. Randy Alcorn wrote, "Saying that joy isn't about being happy is like saying that rain isn't wet or ice isn't cold."[6] Scripture contains many promises that refute the false dichotomy between joy and happiness. Read Psalm 68:3; Proverbs 10:28; 15:15; James 5:13. God created us to desire happiness. The gospel is now and always has been good news.

Life Line

God intends good things for his children, on earth as well as in heaven.

THE ONLY THING YOU NEED TO REMEMBER TODAY

[Jesus said,] "If you love me, show it by doing what I've told you. I will talk to the Father, and he'll provide you another Friend so that you will always have someone with you. This Friend is the Spirit of Truth. The godless world can't take him in because it doesn't have eyes to see him, doesn't know what to look for. But you know him already because he has been staying with you, and will even be in you!"

JOHN 14:15-17, MSG

MY HUSBAND HAD THE DAY OFF and offered to run errands so I could write. The list I ticked off was long: driving my mom to her hair appointment, picking up event tickets, stopping by the driver's license bureau, grabbing a gift for one of the kids. As he headed out the door, I hollered, "Can you get the dry cleaning too? And don't forget the milk!"

Mike stopped and gave me The Look, the one that said, *I will never remember all that; please write it down.* So I sent him a text. But I still forgot the one thing I needed most: stamps.

To manage my too-much-to-do life, I make lists, print and digital. I delegate tasks to my spouse and other willing victims. I update my iPhone and my daily planner. *And I still can't remember it all.*

We all have these to-do lists in life, lists that seem longer than we can ever tackle. But what if we chose to set that all aside? What if we forgot everything needing to be done today and simply remembered the one most important thing?

Several years ago, I was visiting my friend Cynthia when her husband, Bob, entered the room. Bob had been diagnosed with Alzheimer's, and Cynthia had recently left a longtime pastoral position she loved to care for him full-time.

"Have you seen my wife?" Bob questioned me, gazing past Cynthia.

Without hesitation, his wife of forty-five years replied calmly, "She had to go to the store, Bob, but she'll be back soon. And she loves you."

Reassured, he turned away, but I looked at my friend, stricken. "He no longer knows you?"

"No," she replied, "and it's devastating. But I still know him."

Cynthia didn't stop loving and caring for Bob when severe cognitive impairment robbed him of his memories of their marriage.[1]

As I observed this demonstration of sacrificial love, I recalled where Cynthia first learned it: the pages of the book that's the greatest love story ever told.

The Old Testament tells the story of Yahweh's covenantal, redemptive love for his people—a rebellious, stubborn, shortsighted tribe who experienced divine provision again and again, only to be afflicted with a deadly disease of the human condition: cognitive spiritual impairment.

As Moses was readying the Israelites to cross the Jordan River, he didn't provide them with a list of new instructions to follow in the land Yahweh was giving them. Instead, he commanded them to remember what God had done for them in the past.

"Watch out! Be careful never to forget what you yourself
have seen. Do not let these memories escape from your
mind as long as you live! And be sure to pass them on to
your children and grandchildren. Never forget the day when
you stood before the LORD your God at Mount Sinai, where
he told me, 'Summon the people before me, and I will
personally instruct them. Then they will learn to fear me as
long as they live, and they will teach their children to fear
me also.'"[2]

If you're feeling overwhelmed by all you need to accomplish, it's
fine to make a list. Write it down, set it aside, check the items off later.

But, friend, you really need to remember only one thing.

Whatever our age, many of us suffer from cognitive spiritual
impairment. In the press of life's constant problems, we forget who
our Father is and all he's done for us in the past. We forget the one
who loves us most. We behave as if he's absent from our lives.

Yet he knows us, and he is caring for us even when we're
unaware of his presence.

If you don't see him at work in your life right now, if you're not
hearing his voice, don't mistake his seeming silence for his absence.
He has not forgotten you, and he never will. The chapter of your
story that you're living right now is not the final word. God is still
writing the book of your life, and as the Author, he has plans for
you beyond what you can imagine.

Recall with a grateful heart what he's done for you in the past,
and as you do, take courage in his plans for your future. If you forget everything else you need to do today, remember this one thing:
God knows you, he loves you, and he is *for* you.

And that's a fact I hope we never forget.

Points of Connection

1. Using a concordance, do a word study on the many passages
   in Scripture that command us to remember. Here are a few
   good places to begin: 1 Chronicles 16:12; Ecclesiastes 12:1;
   John 14:26; 1 Corinthians 11:24. How does it encourage you
   to know that Jesus promised the presence of the Counselor,
   the Holy Spirit, to help his disciples remember all that he had
   taught them?

2. When have you mistaken God's silence for his absence? Ask the
   Holy Spirit to remind you of the ways he has provided for you
   in the past even when you were unaware of his hand at work.

3. If you're feeling overwhelmed by all you need to accomplish
   or remember, take courage from this promise from the Old
   Testament: "I am overwhelmed with joy in the LORD my
   God! For he has dressed me with the clothing of salvation and
   draped me in a robe of righteousness" (Isaiah 61:10, NLT). We
   are covered in Christ's righteousness when we believe in him
   (2 Corinthians 5:21). How does this promise spark joy in your
   heart today?

Life Line

If you forget all else, remember this: God knows you, he loves you, and
he will never, ever leave you.

FROM DESPERATE TO DAUGHTER

[Jesus] said to her, "Daughter, your faith has made you
well. Go in peace. Your suffering is over."

MARK 5:34, NLT

IT'S BEEN OVER TWENTY YEARS, but I can still recall the sound of the small voice reaching out to us from the back seat of the car.

"Mr. Rowe, what can I call you?"

Puzzled, my husband half turned to where Sarah sat behind us, next to our biological daughter, Amber. Sarah and her younger brother had recently come to live with us in foster care when their own parents were no longer able to care for them.

"I still have a father who's alive somewhere," she said hesitantly, "and Amber calls you Dad, but I don't know what I should call you. What did people in the Bible call their parents?"

We couldn't see Sarah's face in the dim light, but we could hear the yearning in her voice. Whose daughter was she now? What was her place in this new world where home, community, and relationships had all been altered?

I often think of Sarah when I read the account of the two

daughters recorded in three of the Gospels.[1] A bleeding, desperate woman presses through the crowd to extract healing power from Jesus while he is on his way to heal another man's daughter.

While often told separately, the stories are interconnected. The healing of the daughter of Jairus, a ruler in the local synagogue, is embedded within the larger story of the hemorrhagic woman, one whose chronic bodily discharge has rendered her untouchable and therefore "unclean" by those in her community.[2] She has been suffering for twelve years, as long as Jairus's daughter has been alive. The woman's past has been decimated; the girl's future is at risk. One has no one to advocate for her; the other has an attentive father.

Yet in the presence of Jesus a miracle happens, the only Gospel miracle that apparently takes Jesus by surprise. When the woman reaches out to clutch the hem of Jesus' garment,[3] he insists she reveal herself. For a woman considered ritually unclean by her culture, touching a holy man violated the boundaries of social convention. Yet Jesus demanded she come out of hiding so that he could affirm rather than accuse her.

"Daughter, your faith has made you well," he said. "Go in peace. Your suffering is over."[4]

Augustine once wrote that flesh presses, but faith touches. Jesus knew the difference and applauded the desperately ill woman for her audacious faith.

More stunning still is the descriptor Jesus used just prior to his declaration of healing. He called the woman *daughter*, the only time Scripture records Jesus using this relational word directly to an individual. Once on the fringes of the crowd, she is now welcomed into the family of God. Jesus was interested in restoring her socially as well as healing her physically.

The account of the two daughters has much to teach us. We

weren't created to live in isolation but community. As daughters of our heavenly Father, we have a responsibility to care for those on the margins of society as Jesus did. No one is beyond the reach of his grace.

And nothing is to be gained by hiding from him. Evasiveness comes naturally to humans. Only three chapters into the Old Testament, God confronts our first parents when he discovers them hiding among the trees.[5] The bleeding woman's intent was to approach Jesus surreptitiously, but Jesus brought her into the open to release her from shame.

Whether it's our past that needs healing or our future that's at risk, Jesus is present in our situation.

The woman endured chronic suffering and consistent isolation that lasted twelve years. Jairus's daughter had only experienced a dozen years of life and would have no future if Jesus did not restore her. Yet Jesus healed them both—and did so immediately. He restored the girl to physical life and placed her back into the welcoming arms of her family. He restored the suffering woman who had been treated as though she were dead: rejected by her community and pushed out of relationship. Each received a miracle.

Do you know someone who needs Jesus' transforming touch today? Maybe even you?

On that night when our new daughter, Sarah, asked my husband what she should call him, Mike explained that children in the first century often called their papa "Abba," the affectionate term Jesus used for his Father.

A pause. "May I call you Abba?" Sarah asked tentatively.

I could hear the emotion in Mike's voice as he answered, "I'd love that, Sarah. May I call you Daughter?"

And I could hear the smile in hers as she said, "I'd like that."

Points of Connection

1. Our relationship with our earthly father can greatly affect how we view God as our heavenly Father. If you had a loving father who was attentive and present in your life, how has that helped you trust God? If your relationship was distant or even nonexistent, what have been the challenges you've faced in your faith relationship?

2. Sometimes suffering can act as our chauffeur, driving us to God. Have you found this to be true? Do you know others who have turned away from God instead because of pain and loss? How do we best care for them?

3. As time permits, look up the following Scriptures about suffering: Isaiah 53:4; John 11:35; 2 Corinthians 4:17; 12:7; 1 Peter 5:7; Revelation 2:9-10. How do these passages help reframe our view of suffering in the light of God's promises?

LifeLine

God did not create us to live in isolation but in community. In his presence, we are beloved daughters.

AND NOW, A FINAL WORD
(OR FIVE)

*"Leave her alone," said Jesus. "Why are you bothering her? She has done a
beautiful thing to me. The poor you will always have with you, and you can help
them any time you want. But you will not always have me. She did what she
could. She poured perfume on my body beforehand to prepare for my burial."*

MARK 14:6-8

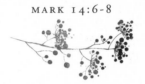

RUTH BELL GRAHAM FAMOUSLY chose a tongue-in-cheek epitaph
for her simple gravestone in Charlotte, North Carolina: *End of
construction—Thank you for your patience.* Eight simple words first
spoken with a grin and a wink, now engraved in stone.

For years, I've joked that I only need three words on my final
resting place: *She meant well.* My last apology to the world for anything I'll have left undone, unspoken, or unintentionally messed
up. A perfectionist by nature, I rarely feel I've done enough. A
spiritual director once told me bluntly, "You apologize more than
anyone I've ever met." (I apologized to her immediately.) So let's
just get this out of the way: I'm sorry for anything this book has
failed to cover!

If you knew that a phone conversation, family meal, or letter to your loved ones was going to be your last, what would you want to communicate? In a few moments, you'll close this book and the connection we've had will end. You've stayed with me through all these pages as we've journeyed together, yet there's still so much I want to tell you. It's as if you've come to visit me at Peace Ridge, and as you wave good-bye, I want to press into your hands courage for the journey ahead, along with a cold drink and a sack lunch.

You've got decisions to make as you travel the twisting road of everyday faith. Can I tell you what I learned the hard way—that the hard choice is so often the right choice? It's harder to be active than to remain passive. It's more difficult to receive than to give. It takes energy and commitment to be a shaper in this world and not a consumer only. You're making those tough choices already; I'm sure you are.

You've got prayer concerns—lots of them. You know the best prayer Jesus taught us to pray—*Your will be done*—but may I offer you another? *Lord, let me be useful in your hands.* It's the prayer that never fails. To become the answer to someone else's prayers is to live a life of rich purpose.

Pastor Bryan Loritts once told university students, "If we're not careful, we can reduce God into being our cosmic concierge, who exists so that I can pull off my best life now. God is not our administrative assistant. He is the CEO of our lives. . . . If God were to answer all of your prayers from the last twelve months—every last one of them—would *the* world change? Or just *your* world?"[1]

You've got regrets in your rearview mirror, and you're likely staring through the windshield at traffic jams ahead. Detours, roadblocks, accidents you can't see coming. Disappointments that won't feel like his appointments for your life. Your own mess-ups and mistakes. They stink, but in God's upside-down Kingdom, nothing is wasted. Manure creates rich fertilizer for the future. (I'm the daughter of a farmer—trust me on this.)

And if some of the road signs that disturb you are the signs of aging, that's normal. You're grateful for the privilege of growing older, but who *is* this stranger staring back at you from the mirror? I'm there too. "We have this treasure in jars of clay," Paul wrote to the Corinthians.[2] It's important to take care of our health, but when we obsess about the state of the jar, we lose focus on the treasure within.

One more advisory for the journey? Keep your travel plans flexible. Jesus is the one true way to heaven, but once you're aimed in his direction, you'll find there's more than one right way to manage life along the way. Mrs. Denhart taught me in the first grade that 2 + 2 = 4, but so does 3 + 1. Walk around that situation vexing you, and pray it through from a different angle of vision. Maybe the way your spouse or coworker or kid is handling it might just work after all.

When a woman busted into a gathering of men in Bethany, where Jesus was present, she didn't ask permission to do what she came to do. In her hands was a bottle of very expensive perfume worth a year's wages; in her heart, the boldness to spill it. While the astonished men watched in disapproval, she poured the fragrant oil over Jesus' head—a priestly anointing,[3] the anointing of a body for burial. As my pastor, Chris, once put it, "365 days of work for one minute of an act of worship."[4]

Into the scolding came the voice of the Savior: "Leave her alone. Why are you bothering her? She has done a beautiful thing to me." And a moment later, Jesus spoke the words that ensured her act would be remembered and discussed throughout the world wherever the Good News is preached. "She did what she could."[5]

She did what she could. She. Did. What. She. Could. Five simple words that honored a selfless act of love. Five simple words that silenced the critics.

The same five words that I choose as my new epitaph for when my journey ends.

As eager as Jesus must have been to return to his Father in heaven, it had to hurt deeply when the moment came to leave the disciples he so dearly loved. But you know what, friends? He did not leave any of us alone to fend for ourselves. We have the Holy Spirit, and we have each other.

May we walk well together on life's journey with purpose, prayer, intentionality, and most of all, love. Let's do what we can to support, encourage, and challenge each other for as long as we can.

Starting here, starting now, in this beautiful life we share.

Points of Connection

1. The Bible is packed with promises God has made to his people, but one thing we're not assured is length of years. Whether you're twenty-five, forty-five, or seventy-five, how can you live each day so that Jesus might one day say of you, "She did what she could"?

2. Sometimes our actions are right even when our intentions are unclear. Did the woman who anointed Jesus' head with oil know that his death was imminent? Regardless of her conscious motivation, "her loving act served the purpose Jesus assigned it."[6] Can you think of instances when you were uncertain of how your actions would be perceived, but conviction compelled you forward? How does it help to know that we serve a loving heavenly Father who can sort out our hearts?

3. If your deeds were to be discussed around the world, how would you wish to be remembered?

LifeLine

What do you hold in your hands and your heart today? Do you have the boldness to spill it out in love and service so it may be said of you, "She did what she could"?

Acknowledgments

IF I WERE EVER TO ACCEPT AN OSCAR on national television, I'd be the one whipping out a fistful of note cards only to have the orchestra drown out my torrent of words long before I was finished. Writing a book is unlike accepting an award except for one thing: There are so many people to thank—not out of obligation but from the depths of a grateful, grateful heart.

My beloved mother, Eunice Thorson Wallem, passed away just a few months before this book's release. While Mom didn't live to hold my book in her hands, her sacrificial love and servant's heart is reflected on every page. Mom was the first one to take my writing seriously, sitting down to her typewriter many evenings to transcribe the penciled scrawls of a third grader into neat pages to mail to the editors of children's magazines. Mom and Dad took me to the library every Friday night to meet my insatiable love of books. And as a ninety-four-year-old, Mom made meals, vacuumed rugs, and emptied the dishwasher for our household day after day so I could type the lessons of a lifetime. This is her book, too.

Don Pape, if I wrote fiction, you'd be the heroic protagonist of my novel. Unknown to me, you were one of the maybe twenty-nine people reading my blog that spring of 2017, and I'll never forget the message you sent telling me I had the chops to write to a wide spectrum of women. Your belief that I had something worth saying has changed my life. Thank you for becoming not only my publisher but our trusted friend.

Caitlyn Carlson, if I ever write that novel, I'll model the heroine after you. When Don said that NavPress was seeking fine dining from their writers rather than fast food, I could not have asked for a better master chef as an editor. I prepared and plated the words, but you were the one who expertly advised me to add meat here or remove fat there. You stirred, seasoned, tasted, and pronounced it good. Will you please edit the other parts of my life as well?

Elizabeth Schroll, copy editor, and **Olivia Eldredge** in operations, thank you for coming alongside me with the savvy smarts and skills you share with every NavPress author. You leave everything you touch better than you found it.

The alliance team at Tyndale: **Robin Bermel,** marketing lead, **Whitney Harrison,** product development manager, and alliances director **Linda Schmitt:** Y'all have been my dream team. You invest personally and professionally in your authors, and I am deeply grateful to be one of them. **Jackie Nuñez,** your cover design is a gift from the Creator himself. I am awed by your talent. And to the rest of the team in public relations, production, sales, and distribution, please know your work is so highly valued. This book-child gestated in my soul, but you brought it to life. Special thanks to **Stephanie Rische** and the **prayer team at Tyndale** for faithfully remembering me before our Father.

To the twelve: Jan, Cindy, Amber, Miriam, Lynne, Christy, Debbie, Joleen, Lesley, Pam, Valerie, and Sharon. Thank you for serving as the spiritual midwives who prayed these words from conception to delivery and have shared them with others. How blessed I am to have you as lifelong friends!

To **Jim and Mary Whitmer:** For nearly twenty years, you generously shared your extraordinary gifts in photography and web design with me. This book was born from a blog site that never would have existed without you. Only God can number the lives you continue to impact around the world.

To the women of **Trinity Church** in Nashua, New Hampshire; **Osterville Baptist** on Cape Cod; and **First Baptist** of Wheaton, Illinois: You partnered with me in over forty years of pastoral ministry to other women. So much of what I share in these pages is what we learned together. Some ministry teams are for a season, while others (**WACOS**, I'm looking at you) are for a lifetime. I'm also deeply grateful for being so warmly embraced by our new church family at **Long's Chapel** in Waynesville, North Carolina. You define true Southern hospitality by the way you care for others in Jesus' name.

Authors who have influenced other writers are typically relegated to footnote status, but there are four women of my generation whose books and personal encouragement have fed my soul for decades. Their work has a place of honor on my bookshelves.

Lucinda Secrest McDowell: The spiritual impact of your fifteen books is second only to the singular influence you've had on my life as my longtime ministry colleague, prayer partner, and best friend. I'm continually in awe of your endless energy, giftedness, and intentional investment in the lives of hundreds of other writers.

Karen Mains: The breadth of your intellect and the depth of your literary talent have inspired me since I first came to faith. I was stunned to discover a Christian writer with a reverence for Scripture coupled with a passion for global engagement long before it entered the mainstream.

Beth Moore: There truly are not words sufficient to express my appreciation for your teaching and writing. Just as I sat under your ministry and my daughter did after me, I pray my granddaughters can grow under your tutelage as well. Thank you for believing in me during the darkest of days years ago, and for your empathy and understanding. And for Babe's Chicken T-shirts and NOLA beignets in happier times!

Gail MacDonald: I'm not sure Mike and I would have thrived in pastoral ministry in New England without you and Gordon. The two of you are a uniquely gifted ministry couple who have demonstrated to generations of us what it's like to live as mercied people. Having you as my mentor and cheerleader has been one of the greatest privileges of my life.

In memory of four deeply loved friends who enthusiastically supported my writing but did not live to its publication: **Esther Peterson,** my Wheaton College coworker who was one of the first to subscribe to my blog. **Margie Watterson,** who radiated sunshine across the aisle at Tyndale and would have been the first with her hand in the air to work with me on this book. **Kathy Tuttle Smith,** whose prayers sustained me since our freshman year in college. Kathy was right—nothing is a long shot if God is in it. And to my kindred-spirit friend **Catherine Reynolds,** who I suspect is leading the hosts of heaven right now in her famous happy dance.

Some women long for a sister their entire lives. I have been blessed with seven through birth and marriage: **Cindy, Jody, Susan, Sherry, Linda, Lori,** and **Christine**. I am so thankful we are sisters in Christ, too, so that our adventures together will continue into eternity. And in memory of **Jeannine:** our beloved oldest sister who outraced us all on the quick race Home. No one would have been more supportive of this book. I'm so thankful we will see you again one day soon, Nene.

Special appreciation to my amazing brother, **Dan,** whose quiet demeanor belies a prodigious intellect coupled with deep faith. You've always been available to talk, Dan, and I talk a *lot*. I can't thank you enough for the personal interest you and Jody have taken in my work.

The orchestra has been playing for several minutes already, but I've saved for last those who will always be first in my life: my husband, children, and grandchildren.

Mike, you read every word of this book not once but many times. You have always believed in me when I never believed in myself. As a pastor and shepherd, you've invested your life in helping people grow while never seeking the spotlight, preferring to let others shine instead. I love you with all my heart, and I thank God every day for this incredible life we share.

Adam and **Liz, Amber** and **Ben,** and **Jordan:** Your dad and I could not be more grateful for the outstanding adults you have become. You're not only our children but our very best friends. Thank you for your thoughtful advice, practical helps, and endless encouragement as I wrote our book. I am so proud of each of you, and of your bonus sibs, **Sarah** and **Matt,** too.

And to our grandchildren: **Libby, Everett, Truman, Elin,** and **Rosemary**. I cannot imagine our lives without you. You are little now, but I hope that when you read these words someday, they'll help you grasp the deep love of God. I pray that long after your Baba and Mormor have departed this planet for Home, you'll carry on our family's mission to love God and serve his people.

Without **readers,** an author's words feed no one. I am deeply thankful for each one, old friends and new, who thoughtfully interact with these pages. If you have purchased this book, posted on social media, or written a review, you have been part of the miracle of taking this humble meal of loaves and fish and distributing it to feed a multitude. *Thank you.*

> By day the LORD directs his love,
>   at night his song is with me—
>   a prayer to the God of my life.

PSALM 42:8

Notes

INTRODUCTION
1. Ecclesiastes 4:9, NLT.

PART I: THE INNER JOURNEY
1. Philippians 2:4, NLT. Emphasis mine.
2. John Macmurray, *Reason and Emotion* (London: Faber and Faber, 1935), 49.
3. Quoted in J. E. Huckabee, *Pursuing Peace: Discovering God's Peace in a Stressful Life* (Bloomington, IN: WestBow Press, 2013), 92.

REFLECTION 1: TOO MUCH TO DO
1. Sue Bender, *Plain and Simple: A Woman's Journey to the Amish* (San Francisco: HarperOne, 1995), 136.
2. Sheryl Sandberg, *Lean In: Women, Work, and the Will to Lead* (New York: Alfred A. Knopf, 2013), 121.

REFLECTION 3: WHEN YOU DON'T FEEL GOOD ENOUGH
1. *This Is Us*, season 2, episode 1, "A Father's Advice," directed by Ken Olin, written by Dan Fogelman, aired September 26, 2017, on NBC.

REFLECTION 4: SHEDDING THE SHAME
1. *Merriam-Webster*, s.v. "shame (*n.*)," accessed October 23, 2019, https://www .merriam-webster.com/dictionary/shame.
2. To view this painting, see https://globalworship.tumblr.com/post /135464914135/virgin-mary-consoles-eve-advent-song-painting.
3. Genesis 3:15.
4. Luke 1:26-38.
5. John 13:3; 17:2.
6. Derek Kidner, *Genesis: An Introduction and Commentary* (Downers Grove, IL: InterVarsity, 1967), 70.
7. 1 Corinthians 15:25.
8. Acts 1:8; Matthew 10:1; Mark 3:15; 6:7; Luke 10:19.

9. Matthew 1:23.
10. Romans 16:20.

REFLECTION 5: HOLDING PEACE
1. Exodus 14:13-14, NLT.
2. Exodus 14:14, NKJV.
3. 1 Thessalonians 5:24.
4. Ephesians 3:16-19.
5. Deuteronomy 29:29.

REFLECTION 6: WHEN JOY ELUDES YOU
1. Galatians 5:22.
2. Henri J. M. Nouwen, *You Are the Beloved: Daily Meditations for Spiritual Living* (New York: Convergent, 2017), 169.
3. Amy Carmichael, *Thou Givest . . . They Gather: Truths Gleaned from the Word of God* (Fort Washington, PA: CLC Publications, 2013), chap. 5.
4. Walter Chalmers Smith, "Immortal, Invisible, God Only Wise," 1867.
5. John 16:22-24, MSG.
6. Isaac Watts (lyrics), "Joy to the World," 1719, public domain.

REFLECTION 7: COPING WITH CRITICISM WITHOUT GETTING BURNED
1. 1 Peter 3:9, NLT.
2. Numbers 14:5.
3. Amy Carmichael, *If* (Fort Washington, PA: CLC Publications, 2011), 36.

REFLECTION 8: FINDING PEACE IN THE MIDST OF PAIN
1. 1 Peter 4:12, NLT.
2. Matthew 26; Mark 14; Luke 22.
3. Luke 22:44.
4. Karen Mains, *Comforting One Another: In Life's Sorrows* (Nashville: Thomas Nelson, 1997), 132.
5. 2 Corinthians 11:21-33.
6. 2 Corinthians 12:7.
7. Proverbs 26:9.
8. 1 Corinthians 12:7.
9. 2 Corinthians 12:9.
10. Oswald Chambers, *My Utmost for His Highest* (Grand Rapids, MI: Discovery House, 2017), November 5.

REFLECTION 9: WHERE DO YOU GO TO GET WARM?
1. 2 Corinthians 1:3-4.

2. David and Nancy Guthrie, *When Your Family's Lost a Loved One: Finding Hope Together* (Carol Stream, IL: Focus on the Family, 2008), 24.
3. Romans 12:15.
4. Intermountain Medical Center, "Engaging Family in Care of Hospitalized Loved Ones Enhances Healing, Reduces Readmission Rates," *ScienceDaily*, February 12, 2018, https://www.sciencedaily.com /releases/2018/02/180212100615.htm.
5. Romans 8:28, ESV.
6. Gail MacDonald, *In His Everlasting Arms: Learning to Trust God in All Circumstances* (Ann Arbor, MI: Servant Publications, 2000), 196.
7. See John 14:16, 26; 15:26; and 16:7 in the KJV. Years ago, I heard of a church in Texas with a ministry to women called "ComfortHer." I love this.

REFLECTION 10: GOD WRITES STRAIGHT BY BROKEN LINES

1. Ann Voskamp, *The Broken Way: A Daring Path into the Abundant Life* (Grand Rapids, MI: Zondervan, 2016), 25.
2. 2 Kings 5:1-19.
3. Colossians 3:13.
4. Isaiah 40:4.

PART II: THE INTENTIONAL JOURNEY

1. Catherine B. Eagan and Marcia O. Levin, *The Irish Book of Days* (Fairfield, CT: Hugh Lauter Levin Associates, 1994).
2. 1 Corinthians 4:5.
3. As quoted in Gail MacDonald, *High Call, High Privilege: A Pastor's Wife Speaks to Every Woman in a Place of Responsibility* (Peabody, MA: Hendrickson, 1998), 139.

REFLECTION 11: FORMED AND FILLED

1. Genesis 1:1-31.
2. With appreciation to Dr. Mitchell Kim, course on Genesis, Wheaton College Graduate School, 2014.
3. Jeremiah 29:11; Ephesians 1:11.
4. Acts 17:24-27; Ephesians 2.
5. Romans 12:2; 1 Corinthians 15:51-54.
6. John 15:2; Colossians 1:6, 10.
7. Colossians 1:15.
8. Matthew 22:37-39.
9. John 3:16.

REFLECTION 12: THE FOCUSED LIFE

1. Luke 19:10, author's paraphrase.

2. Mark 1:35-38.
3. Psalm 90:10, KJV.
4. As quoted in Guy Chmieleski; "Be Present," *Catalyst*, October 6, 2011, http://faithoncampus.com/blog/catalyst-andy-stanley-be-present/.

REFLECTION 13: CONFIDENCE IN YOUR CALLING
1. 1 Samuel 10:1-27.
2. Max Lucado, *Outlive Your Life: You Were Made to Make a Difference* (Nashville: Thomas Nelson, 2010), 3.
3. Genesis 1:31.

REFLECTION 14: YOUR LACK DOES NOT DEFINE YOU
1. Exodus 21; Leviticus 25.
2. Read her story in 2 Kings 4:1-7.
3. Job 16:20; Psalm 62:8.
4. Exodus 4:2, NCV.
5. John 15:5; Romans 8:26.

REFLECTION 15: STEPPING IN, STOOPING DOWN, LIFTING UP
1. Steve Wiens, *Whole: Restoring What Is Broken in Me, You, and the Entire World* (Colorado Springs, CO: NavPress, 2017), xiv.
2. We're not alone in this. *Merriam-Webster* defines *compassion fatigue* as "apathy or indifference toward the suffering of others as the result of overexposure to tragic news stories and images and the subsequent appeals for assistance." *Merriam-Webster*, s.v. "compassion fatigue (*n.*)," accessed October 24, 2019, https://www.merriam-webster.com/dictionary/compassion%20fatigue.
3. Luke 10:30-37.
4. Exodus 2:6.
5. 2 Chronicles 28:15.
6. Acts 28:2.
7. *Mister Rogers' Neighborhood.*

REFLECTION 16: FAST FOOD AND THE THEOLOGY OF WAITING
1. Psalm 37:7.
2. Ruth 3:18, KJV.
3. Romans 12:12.
4. Romans 8:25.
5. Bible Hub, s.v. "5281. hupomoné," accessed November 7, 2019, https://biblehub.com/greek/5281.htm.
6. J. R. R. Tolkien, *The Lord of the Rings*, one vol. (London: HarperCollins, 2005), 77.

REFLECTION 17: WHEN YOU THOUGHT YOU WERE DOING IT RIGHT

1. Attributed to Maya Angelou.
2. Jeremiah 29:11.
3. On several visits I've taken to Bethlehem, guides pointed to reconstructed homes from the first century with cave-like rooms attached to the main dwelling to house animals. Scripture indicates only that Jesus was laid in a manger.
4. John Ortberg, *What Is God's Will for My Life?* (Carol Stream, IL: Tyndale, 2016), 12.
5. 2 Chronicles 16:9.

REFLECTION 18: FEELING LIKE A PHONY

1. Sheryl Sandberg, *Lean In: Women, Work, and the Will to Lead* (New York: Alfred A. Knopf, 2013), 28.
2. Pauline Rose Clance and Suzanne Ament Imes, "The Impostor Phenomenon in High Achieving Women: Dynamics and Therapeutic Intervention," *Psychotherapy* 15, no. 3 (Fall 1978), 241–247.
3. Stephanie O'Brien, "Beat Imposter Syndrome: How to Stand Firm in Who God Says You Are When You Feel Like a Phony," *Christianity Today*, October 19, 2017, https://www.christianitytoday.com/women-leaders/2017/october/beat -imposter-syndrome.html.
4. Sandberg, *Lean In*, 29.
5. John 1:12; Ephesians 1:5.
6. Romans 15:7; Colossians 2:9-10.
7. Genesis 1:27; Romans 6:6.
8. Ephesians 2:10, NLT.
9. For more on this topic, I highly recommend Beth Moore's *So Long, Insecurity: You've Been a Bad Friend to Us* (Carol Stream, IL: Tyndale, 2010).
10. 1 Thessalonians 5:24. Emphasis mine.

REFLECTION 19: ON BEING SECOND

1. Inspired by the subtitle of this book: Clay Scroggins, *How to Lead When You're Not in Charge: Leveraging Influence When You Lack Authority* (Grand Rapids, MI: Zondervan, 2017).
2. Acts 4:36.
3. Constance D. Rogers, *Galatians: Free to Love* (unpublished, 2018). Used with permission.
4. Acts 13:1-5.
5. Acts 9:26-27.
6. Acts 15:36-39.
7. Name has been changed.
8. Hebrews 12:11.
9. Proverbs 15:33.
10. Hebrews 13:17.

11. Timothy Keller, *The Freedom of Self-Forgetfulness: The Path to True Christian Joy* (Leyland, UK: 10Publishing, 2012), 32.

12. James 4:10; 1 Peter 5:6.

REFLECTION 20: WHAT I SAW AT THE GYM ON MULBERRY STREET

1. Philippians 4:8.
2. Emphasis mine.
3. Inspired by Dr. Seuss, *And to Think That I Saw It on Mulberry Street* (New York: Vanguard, 1937).
4. Kate B. Wilkinson (lyrics), "May the Mind of Christ, My Savior," 1925, public domain.

REFLECTION 21: WHAT WE CAN'T SEE

1. Name has been changed.

REFLECTION 22: NO MORE FALSE FACE

1. Robyn Turk, "Fake It Till You Make It!," *Daily Mail*, November 29, 2018, https://www.dailymail.co.uk/femail/article-6435173/People-taking-Instagram-photos-inside-fake-private-jet-interior-inside-store.html.
2. John 1:47, KJV.
3. John 1:47, MSG.
4. Luke 16:10, NLT.
5. David Pratt, comp., *The Impossible Takes Longer: The 1,000 Wisest Things Ever Said by Nobel Prize Laureates* (New York: Walker & Company, 2007), 17.

REFLECTION 23: AGING GRATEFULLY

1. 2 Corinthians 4:16.
2. (Well, sort of, sometimes, if I feel like it.)
3. Tim Kimmel, *Legacy of Love: A Plan for Parenting on Purpose* (Portland, OR: Multnomah, 1989), 23.
4. John 14:12. For a thorough treatment of what Jesus may have meant by this statement, I recommend Jan de Chambrier, *Greater Things Than These: Practicing What Jesus Preached* (Palmyra, PA: Healing Tree International, 2019).

PART III: THE RELATIONAL JOURNEY

1. David G. Benner, *Sacred Companions: The Gift of Spiritual Friendship & Direction* (Downers Grove, IL: IVP, 2004), 41.

REFLECTION 24: KINDRED SPIRITS

1. L. M. Montgomery, *The Annotated Anne of Green Gables* (New York: Oxford University Press, 1997), 105.

2. Montgomery, *The Annotated Anne of Green Gables*, 138.
3. Elliot Engel, "Of Male Bondage," quoted in Dee Brestin, *The Friendships of Women* (Wheaton, IL: Victor Books, 1988), 17.
4. Ecclesiastes 4:9-12.
5. C. S. Lewis, *The Four Loves*, reissue edition (San Francisco: HarperOne, 2017), 57.
6. Matthew 6:33, CEV.
7. John 15:14.
8. Sarah Orne Jewett, "The Country of the Pointed Firs," *Atlantic Monthly*, vol. 78.

REFLECTION 25: MAGGIE'S TEN COMMANDMENTS OF FRIENDSHIP

1. Exodus 20:3-17.
2. Psalm 62:5-6.
3. Proverbs 19:4, 6.
4. Proverbs 11:13.
5. 1 Thessalonians 5:11.
6. Philippians 2:4.
7. Proverbs 18:13; James 1:19.
8. Proverbs 20:6.
9. 1 Corinthians 13:4.
10. Ephesians 4:29.
11. 1 Corinthians 12:26.

REFLECTION 26: JUDGING. NOT.

1. John 7:24, NLT.
2. 1 Corinthians 5.
3. Galatians 6:1.

REFLECTION 27: PRICKLY PEOPLE (AND OTHER PROBLEMS . . .)

1. Reflection 8.
2. 2 Corinthians 12:7-10.
3. From Charles M. Schulz, *Peanuts*, as quoted in *The 2,320 Funniest Quotes: The Most Hilarious Quips and One-Liners from allgreatquotes.com* (Berkeley, CA: Ulysses Press, 2011), 220.
4. Luke 12:51-52; Romans 12:18.
5. Matthew 7:7, 11; Luke 18:1-8.
6. 2 Corinthians 12:8.
7. 2 Corinthians 12:7.
8. Proverbs 16:18; James 4:6.
9. Beth Moore, *To Live Is Christ: The Life and Ministry of Paul* (Nashville: LifeWay, 1997), Session 10 video.
10. 2 Corinthians 12:9.

11. Hebrews 6:8; 1 Peter 3:9.
12. Robin Abcarian, "Michelle Obama's Stunning Convention Speech: 'When They Go Low, We Go High,'" *Los Angeles Times*, July 25, 2016, https://www.latimes.com/politics/la-na-pol-michelle-speech-20160725-snap-story.html.
13. Romans 5:12-21.
14. 2 Corinthians 5:21.
15. Ephesians 5:20.

REFLECTION 28: FRIENDSHIP FAIL
1. Name has been changed.
2. Michael Finkel, *The Stranger in the Woods: The Extraordinary Story of the Last True Hermit* (New York: Alfred A. Knopf, 2017), 137.
3. Name has been changed.

REFLECTION 29: DOES ANYONE WANT TO MENTOR ME?
1. James 5:10-11.
2. Sheryl Sandberg, *Lean In: Women, Work, and the Will to Lead* (New York: Alfred A. Knopf, 2013), 65.
3. Sandberg, *Lean In*, 67.
4. Wilkinson died in 2018.
5. A. J. Baime with Giannella M. Garrett, "Friends for the Ages: The Power of Cross-Generational, Age-Defying Bonds," *AARP*, June/July 2017, https://www.aarp.org/home-family/friends-family/info-2017/power-of-lasting-friendships.html.

REFLECTION 31: RIDING TANDEM
1. *ESV Study Bible* (Wheaton, IL: Crossway, 2008), 2271, notes on Ephesians 5:21.

REFLECTION 32: PUTTING THE SALSA BACK IN YOUR MARRIAGE
1. Genesis 2:23-25; 1 Corinthians 7:3-5.
2. "As soon as I saw you, I knew a grand adventure was going to happen." Attributed to Winnie the Pooh.

REFLECTION 33: PARTY OF ONE? THIS WAY, PLEASE!
1. 1 Corinthians 7:7-8.
2. Mandy Hale, foreword to Joy Beth Smith, *Party of One: Truth, Longing, and the Subtle Art of Singleness* (Nashville: Thomas Nelson, 2018), xiii.
3. Smith, *Party of One*, 212.
4. Name has been changed.
5. Timothy Keller with Kathy Keller, *The Meaning of Marriage: Facing the Complexities of Commitment with the Wisdom of God* (New York: Riverhead Books, 2011), 198.

REFLECTION 34: CRADLES AND THE CROSS

1. Catherine McNiel, *Long Days of Small Things: Motherhood as a Spiritual Discipline* (Colorado Springs, CO: NavPress, 2017), 4.
2. McNiel, *Long Days*, 9–10.
3. Elisabeth Elliot, *A Chance to Die: The Life and Legacy of Amy Carmichael* (Grand Rapids, MI: Fleming H. Revell, 1987), 183.
4. As quoted in Adele Ahlberg Calhoun, *Spiritual Disciplines Handbook: Practices That Transform Us* (Downers Grove, IL: IVP Books, 2005), 146.

REFLECTION 35: LORD, LET MY KIDS GET CAUGHT

1. Hebrews 12:11, NLT.
2. Matthew 26:31-35; Mark 14:27-31.
3. Matthew 26:70-74.
4. Matthew 26:75.
5. 1 John 1:9.
6. 2 Corinthians 7:8-11.

REFLECTION 36: MORE WAYS THAN ONE TO BE A MOM

1. Ruth 1:16-18.
2. Luke 1:39-45.
3. Judges 4:4-9.
4. Exodus 2:1-10; 5:20-21.
5. Judges 5:7.
6. Numbers 12:1-15.
7. Beth Moore, *Breaking Free: Making Liberty in Christ a Reality in Life* (Nashville, TN: LifeWay Press, 1999), 131.
8. Isaiah 40:11.
9. Larry B. Stammer, "Preaching Abundant Living," *Los Angeles Times*, December 2, 2003, https://www.latimes.com/archives/la-xpm-2003-dec-02-et-stammer2-story .html.

REFLECTION 39: WHAT THE AMISH CAN TEACH US ABOUT HOSPITALITY

1. Names of hosts and hostesses in this reflection have been changed.

REFLECTION 40: OUTLIVING YOUR LIFE

1. Revelation 2:17, NLT. Emphasis added.
2. Romans 1:9, NLT.
3. Philippians 4:1, NLT.
4. Facebook comment left by Wheaton College alumnus at the time of Jimma's passing.

PART IV: THE GOD OF YOUR JOURNEY
1. Read the story in Luke 2:41-52.
2. Leviticus 26:12.
3. David Bradstreet and Steve Rabey, *Star Struck: Seeing the Creator in the Wonder of Our Cosmos* (Grand Rapids, MI: Zondervan, 2016), chap. 12.
4. John 1:14, MSG.

REFLECTION 41: *HEY, THEOPHILUS!* BECOMING A FRIEND OF GOD
1. Mark 14:36; Romans 8:15; Galatians 4:6.
2. John 14:9-11.
3. Matthew 28:20; Philippians 2:7; Hebrews 4:15.
4. Isaiah 41:8; James 2:23.
5. 1 Samuel 13:14; Acts 13:22.
6. Luke 10:1.
7. John 11:3, NLT.
8. Mark 16:9; John 20:11, 14.
9. Romans 5:1-2, NLT.
10. John 15:14-15, MSG.
11. Revelation 3:20, NLT.
12. Oswald Chambers, *My Utmost for His Highest* (New York: Dodd, Mead, & Co., 1956), 335.

REFLECTION 42: SANCTUARY
1. Patricia Cornwell, *Ruth, A Portrait: The Story of Ruth Bell Graham* (New York: Doubleday, 1997), 161.

REFLECTION 43: THE FRAGRANCE OF FAITH
1. "Healthbeat Report: Salty Solutions," ABC7, August 5, 2010, http://abc7chicago .com/archive/7595385/.
2. Alex Murashko, "Megachurch Pastor: Christians Thinking in Secular Way Contribute to Fast Rise of the 'Nones,'" *Christian Post*, May 21, 2014, http:// www.christianpost.com/news/megachurch-pastor-christians-thinking-in-secular -way-contribute-to-fast-rise-of-the-nones-120101/.
3. *Africa Study Bible* (Carol Stream, IL: Oasis International, 2016), African Touch Points: Salt, 1385.
4. John 4:13-14.
5. Matthew 5:13.

REFLECTION 44: GOD SO LOVED THE WORLD. DO WE?
1. "A Letter to President Trump and Congress," WorldRelief.org, February 7, 2018, https://worldrelief.org/blog/a-letter-to-president-trump-and-congress.

2. USCIRF, Twitter post, September 10, 2019, https://twitter.com/USCIRF /status/1171399785384992768.

3. Hebrews 8:10, author's paraphrase.

4. This statement was made in a course on Justice and Faith taught by Karen Romanovich and Sasha Brady at First Baptist Church (Wheaton, IL), September 7, 2014. Used with permission.

5. Matthew 25:40.

6. Scott Sauls, *Befriend: Create Belonging in an Age of Judgment, Isolation, and Fear* (Carol Stream, IL: Tyndale, 2016), 165.

7. Sauls, *Befriend*, 33.

REFLECTION 45: DO I LOVE TO TELL THE STORY?

1. Arabella Katherine Hankey (lyrics), "I Love to Tell the Story," 1866, public domain.

2. Kate Shellnutt, "Half of Millennial Christians Say It's Wrong to Evangelize," *Christianity Today*, February 6, 2019, https://www.christianitytoday.com /news/2019/february/half-of-millennial-christians-wrong-to-evangelize-barna .html.

3. John 14:6.

4. 2 Peter 2:4-9.

5. Alpha (alphausa.org), Cru (cru.org), and the Billy Graham Evangelistic Association (billygraham.org) provide excellent resources for evangelism, along with many other organizations. For discipleship resources, contact The Navigators (navigators.org).

6. Mark 8:36-37, NLT.

REFLECTION 46: THE PARADOX OF UNANSWERED PRAYER

1. Matthew 7:7-8; Psalm 37:4.

2. Acts 12:1-16.

3. Jeremiah 31:3; John 3:16; Romans 5:8.

4. Psalm 91:15; Luke 11:9; John 15:7.

5. Romans 1:17; Hebrews 11:1.

6. Psalm 88:14.

REFLECTION 47: PAPERWHITES AND PRAYER

1. John 13:7, NLT.

REFLECTION 48: WHAT WAS I THINKING?

1. Job 31:4; 34:21.

2. Psalm 90:4.

3. 1 John 1:9.

4. 1 Peter 2:24, NKJV.

REFLECTION 49: TOO GOOD TO BE TRUE? IT JUST MIGHT BE ANYWAY
1. Psalm 119:71.
2. Hebrews 12:11.
3. Hebrews 13:16.
4. Randy Alcorn, *60 Days of Happiness: Discover God's Promise of Relentless Joy* (Carol Stream, IL: Tyndale, 2016), 235.
5. 1 Corinthians 2:9, NLT.
6. Alcorn, *60 Days of Happiness*, 45.

REFLECTION 50: THE ONLY THING YOU NEED TO REMEMBER TODAY
1. Cynthia Fantasia shares similar stories in her book *In the Lingering Light: Courage and Hope for the Alzheimer's Caregiver* (Colorado Springs, CO: NavPress, 2019).
2. Deuteronomy 4:9-10, NLT.

REFLECTION 51: FROM DESPERATE TO DAUGHTER
1. Matthew 9:18-26; Mark 5:21-43; Luke 8:40-56.
2. Leviticus 15:25-27.
3. On a recent trip to Israel, I learned this quite possibly could have been Jesus' *tallit katan* or prayer shawl, a garment worn by every Jewish man.
4. Mark 5:34, NLT. See also Matthew 9:22 and Luke 8:48.
5. Genesis 3.

REFLECTION 52: AND NOW, A FINAL WORD (OR FIVE)
1. Bryan Loritts, "The Life-Changing Power of Persistent Prayer," chapel address at Cedarville University, December 7, 2016, https://www.cedarville.edu/Chapel/Watch/The-Power-of-Prayer/eIm3goq20ESXKacsSXxOUA?y=4.
2. 2 Corinthians 4:7.
3. Exodus 29:4-7; 2 Kings 9:1-6.
4. Rev. Chris Westmoreland in sermon delivered at Long's Chapel UMC, Waynesville, North Carolina, March 31, 2019.
5. Mark 14:6, 8.
6. *NLT Parallel Study Bible* (Carol Stream, IL: Tyndale, 2011), note on Mark 14:8, 1871.